ZINGERS

25 Real-Life Character Builders

David and Kathy Lynn

Zondervan Publishing House
Grand Rapids, Michigan

ACKNOWLEDGEMENTS

We would like to thank Dallas Sherwood as well as the many other young people who told us their stories. Their insights into the struggles of growing up in today's hurried world made the writing of ZINGERS possible.

Zingers
Copyright © 1990 by David and Kathy Lynn
All rights reserved

Published by Zondervan Publishing House
1415 Lake Drive, S.E., Grand Rapids, Michigan 49506

Library of Congress Cataloging-in-Publication Data

Lynn, David, 1954–
    Zingers : 25 real-life character builders / David Lynn.
       p.   cm.
    Summary: Presents true-to-life problem situations, in such areas
as alcohol, Christianity, drugs, lying, and sexual exploitation, and
asks readers to decide how they should be handled.
    ISBN 0-310-52511-X
    1. Children—conduct of life. 2. Children—Religious life.
[1. Conduct of life. 2. Christian life.] I. Title.
BJ1631.L96   1990
241–dc20   90–34491
                                                                              CIP
                                                                              AC

All Scripture quotations, unless otherwise noted, are taken from the *Holy Bible: New International Version* (North American Edition). Copyright © 1973, 1978, 1984, by the International Bible Society. Used by permission of Zondervan Bible Publishers.

Printed in the United States of America

90 91 92 93 94 / DP / 5 4 3 2 1

ZINGERS
TABLE OF CONTENTS

SECTION ONE: Problem Situation

Your young people will be asked to examine a problem situation, share their feelings about the situation, and decide how the situation should have been handled. Here the young people face true-to-life problem situations that used to be faced by older youth but now confront the nine-to-twelve-year-old.

SECTION TWO: Right or Wrong?

The group is asked to decide whether certain people and their moral acts were right or wrong and why.

SECTION THREE: What Would Christ Do?

The situations here look at common problems-in-living that have no easy answers. Here the group has the chance to offer support and possible Christian coping strategies to young people facing similar situations.

SECTION FOUR: Let's Pretend

These situations ask the young people to make believe they are in tempting or difficult situations that require them to make tough choices. The adult leader is given the opportunity to guide the group as they face these dilemmas.

Index by Topic

Parents of preadolescents can remember only a few years before when they would read a story at bedtime to help put their children to sleep. Now their children tell stories at bedtime that keep these same parents awake. Times have changed. And the changes have affected young people, making it difficult for kids to be kids. Many of the same issues that affected yesterday's adolescents now have an impact on today's preadolescents. Parents who used to be relieved that their child was not yet a teenager now find the years from nine to thirteen nearly as perplexing and bewildering as their parents found their adolescence. Children at this age now face issues like alcohol abuse, rock music, rebellion, dissatisfaction with church, shoplifting, and pornography. So what happened?

The Growing-Up-Too-Fast Syndrome

David Elkind— a developmental psychologist— and other writers have pointed out that children today face enormous pressure to rush through childhood. Younger and younger children are forced prematurely into the world of adulthood. Their childhood years are no longer a guaranteed sanctuary from the pressures and stress of adult life. Talk with elementary school teachers and you may be surprised to hear them discuss childhood stress. The pressures to succeed, the increased competition from organized sports at younger ages, and the uncertainty of family life all are producing symptoms of stress in preadolescent children. Stress signs in children such as headaches, grinding of the teeth, out-of-the-ordinary crying, upset stomachs, and nervous behaviors are commonly reported by elementary and middle school teachers.

There are other signs that children are pressured into growing up too quickly. Look at the dress of children and you will not see much difference between the way children dress, the way teenagers dress, and the way adults dress. Try buying a swimsuit for a ten-year-old girl and you will quickly understand the growing-up-too-fast syndrome. The next time you are at the video rental store, observe the kinds of movies this age group is renting. Or simply talk to a preadolescent and you will find them knowing more about adult issues like homosexuality, abortion, violence, divorce, or abuse than previous generations.

This rush to grow up has blurred the distinction between what it means to be a preadolescent and what it means to be an adolescent. The growing-up-too-fast syndrome has produced an "experimenting-too-soon" phenomenon whereby young people during the preteen years now engage in behaviors normally associated with the teenage years. Nine-to-twelve-year-olds are now more prone to experiment with smoking, sex, delinquency, oppositional behavior toward authority, and alcohol or drug abuse. Not all preadolescents experiment with these behaviors, but they are all exposed to someone who does.

The following diagram illustrates what we think is happening with today's young people.*

AGE	VALUES	BEHAVIORS
1-8		Minimal Departure
9-13		Moderate Departure
14-18		Maximum Departure
19-24		Moderate Departure
25+		Minimal Departure

Children's behavior, until about the age of nine, differs little from the values they have been taught. However, between the ages of nine and thirteen, young people begin to experiment with behaviors that conflict with their values. (We are grateful to the late Hershel Thornburg, a former professor, for his insights into the values-behavior inconsistency problem with young people.) This experimenting-too-soon phenomenon begins so early because in today's world there are so many more opportunities to experiment. Past generations of American youths were presented with a Judeo-Christian moral standard that prevailed throughout society. The home was supported by the church, school, media, and neighborhood in presenting an agreed-upon set of moral standards and behaviors to kids. Today, young people are exposed to a smorgasbord of choices.

Preadolescents are especially affected by this plurality because they have reached an age where they begin to second-guess their parents, teachers, and church leaders' values. They face behavioral choices because of the barrage of pressures pushing them to do things like cheat on a spelling test, shoplift, or drink. We have chosen to call these choices "pressure points" because they place demands on our kids to make immediate decisions of right and wrong without the help and support of societal standards. By adolescence these pressure points have reached their peak, creating a maximum departure between behaviors and values. However, during the career/college years of nineteen to twenty-four, there is less discrepancy between young peoples' values and behaviors. They begin to return to the values taught them by the home and church. By adulthood, most people have returned to their childhood values. This explanation of values and behaviors supports the biblical model of Proverbs 22:6: "Train a child in the way he should go, and when he is old he will not turn from it."

What concerns us here is the preadolescent years, when kids begin to experiment with behaviors inconsistent with the values they have been taught. Research appears to indicate that the greater the inconsistency between values and behaviors, the more likely it is that the young person's values will change to conform with the new behaviors.

Benefits of a Zinger Discussion

You and your group will experience a great many benefits by using Zingers as part of your Christian education. Take a look at the following benefits to see if these are things you want for your group.

1. Zinger discussions diffuse the pressure points of the preadolescent growing-up experience. We as adults must become more intentional in teaching our values to young people so they have a foundation from which to operate when they confront the pressure points. In the past, it was not necessary to teach values regularly and actively because they were absorbed and reinforced by society's Judeo-Christian standards. But with the breakdown of Judeo-Christian values has come an increasing number of values choices and consequently more demanding pressure points.

2. Zinger discussions transfer learning to the real world. The four walls of the church, school, or club provide an artificial world for Christian kids. Within these four walls we sometimes offer simple life solutions that are not realistic or practical. Often the preadolescent does not transfer these simplistic answers to the realities of daily living. As young people move from grade to grade within their Christian education, they often find that what they learn is not related to real-life experiences. When truth learned at church, school, or club does not work in the real world, kids will more readily question and throw out their faith when they are with their friends. What young people need is a Christian education that is relevant to their life experiences.

Kids can best transfer their learning to the real world if group discussions in the classroom setting closely approximate real-life situations, feelings, and issues. When young people encounter similar situations, feelings, or issues in their world, they can then more easily transfer the knowledge and skills they acquired in the classroom setting. The closer the discussions are to true-to-life situations, the more easily the transfer will occur. Zingers have been designed to facilitate this kind of transfer. Based upon real-life stories, Zingers take your kids' world and bring it into the classroom for examination. As a group you then learn to apply God's Word to the realities of their world.

3. Zinger discussions provide a valuable youth/adult learning partnership opportunity. Adults often see preadolescents as recipients of our adult knowledge. We believe that as adults we know what is best for the kids and view our young people as objects or recipients without much to offer. We as adults dominate discussions and other Christian educational experiences with our right answers and spiritual insights. We are like the disciples who shooed the children away from Jesus (Luke 18:15--17). If we see kids only as recipients of our spiritual insights our dialogues with them will quickly become monologues. We will wonder why our youth refuse to "open up" with us. The problem isn't them; the problem is us. Our view of preadolescence has become distorted by our "adultness." What can we do? We, as adults, need to see preadolescents as resources of wisdom and spiritual insight.

Zinger discussions offer you as an adult leader the opportunity to create an adult/youth learning partnership. Practically speaking this can be done through:

(a) Actively listening to your group members as they tell their stories related to the Zinger situation.

(b) Respecting the opinions of all your group members regardless of how off base any of their comments are.

(c) Empathizing with your young people about what it means to be a preadolescent. This can be done by re membering what it was like to be young yourself.

(d) Spending time with young people. Most of your kids spend the majority of their time with kids their own age.

Large classrooms, after-school programs, and organized sports all place kids in situations with their peers. A Zinger discussion allows adults to be actively involved in the lives of kids. Spending time dialoguing with kids about important issues will earn you the right to be heard by them.

4. Zinger discussions provide you with a spiritual gauge of your group. Zinger discussions will help you discover what the kids in your group believe and how they are acting upon their beliefs. This is invaluable for the children's worker who wishes to understand the needs of young people. An effective children's ministry bases itself upon the needs of its young people.

Zinger discussions will also help your kids discover what they believe. Zingers give you an opportunity to engage your kids in dialogue regarding their beliefs and the inconsistency between their beliefs, actions, and God's Word.

5. Zinger discussions encourage positive peer pressure. A guided Zinger discussion gets kids talking with adults and each other and gives them the chance to lead and influence each other in positive directions. To counter the effects of negative peer pressure, use Zingers to create pressure to do what is honoring to God. Your group members can encourage positive behavior and values in one another.

Ingredients for a Good Zinger Discussion

You may be asking yourself why we are recommending a Zinger discussion rather than a Zinger lecture or a Zinger sermon. Why not just read the Zinger and tell the group what they should and should not do?

Research has found that we as adults possess a valuable tool in helping young people learn right from wrong. That tool is dialogue. Zingers allow you to dialogue with young people through a discussion. But good discussions don't just happen—we *make* them happen. To help the group enter into a meaningful, life-changing discussion, you must pay attention to the four ingredients of a good discussion: correct attitude, healthy ground rules, discussion motivators, and perceptive questioning.

Attitude Check

If you believe adults know what is best for kids, then you will have difficulty leading a good Zinger discussion. Why? Because adults do not always know what is best, and kids know it. If adults did know what was best for young people the youth culture would not be in the mess it is today! Viewing young people as the recipients of our good intentions and valuable knowledge only sets us up to be tested by kids. Young people are not stupid. They will see through our patronizing attitudes. What young people need is a youth/adult partnership that communicates an attitude of acceptance and respect. Your group members need to know that their contributions to any discussion are important, that each young person's

opinion is worth hearing and considering. This does not mean every opinion is worth accepting. Affirmation and approval are two very different things. For a good discussion to occur, however, your group members will need to know that whatever they say will not be laughed at, put down, or considered stupid.

In your discussions you will get a number of comments and opinions that are off base. These can be handled in several ways. You can make a mental note of off-base contributions to the discussion, and then when you are wrapping up the discussion or introducing biblical insight into the discussion, you can correct those off-base opinions or present an alternative viewpoint. This needs to be done in a way that does not put down any of your group members. Another way to handle those off-base opinions is to probe them with questions that push the group to think. Again, this must be done in a responsible way so that the group feels safe in continuing to share their personal opinions. Any time the group does not feel safe in sharing their views they will begin to say things that you, the leader, want to hear. You may be satisfied by their spiritual responses, but will the discussion actually produce changed lives?

Zinger Discussion Ground Rules

One of the best ways we have found to build this type of acceptance with and among young people is by creating ground rules that guide your discussion. You can begin your discussion by brainstorming a few rules with your group. It helps to write the rules down and post them for everyone to see, as you may need to refer back to them during the discussion.

Keep the number of ground rules to a minimum. Here are some suggested ones that you may want to incorporate into your rules.

1. "What is said in this room stays in this room." Confidentiality is primary if young people are ever to trust you. If you rush off to tell their parents that they once cheated on a spelling test, you will never see them open up again in your group. Confidentiality should only be broken when young people reveal they are going to do harm to themselves or another person or when someone is harming them.

2. "All opinions are worth hearing." This means no put-downs, laughs, or rude comments. Disagreement about a group member's opinion can be expressed without attacking the person. Keep the discussion focused on the opinion, not on the person expressing it.

3. "There is no such thing as a dumb question." All questions are legitimate. When young people know they can ask their questions without fear, you have earned their trust and respect.

4. "No one can be forced to talk." Give

everyone the right to pass on any question asked of them. This keeps the discussion safe.

5. "Only one person talking at a time." If each person's opinion is worth being heard, the group can demonstrate this practically by actively listening to everyone who talks. Side talk (talking with the person beside you when someone else is trying to speak) is one form of a put-down.

Motivators for Discussion

By using tested leadership discussion skills you can motivate your group to learn by working through a Zinger together. The following are discussion skills that will help you facilitate a healthy discussion.

1. Interacting. It will be difficult for your group to interact positively with each other if they are seated in rows. It will be equally difficult for them to interact if they are scattered throughout the room—some in chairs, a few on a couch, others standing, and the rest on the floor. For optimal interaction ask your group to sit in a circle where each group member can see the faces of all other group members.

The size of the group also affects interaction. As a general rule of thumb, the larger the group, the more likely people will interact. If you find that only a few young people speak, break into smaller groups for a discussion, then come together as a large group for a closure statement.

Encourage all group members to participate in the discussion. When one person (and that includes you) monopolizes the group time, the discussion gets bogged down quickly. If you are having difficulty involving everyone, have a Nerf ball or other soft foam ball on hand. Whenever the ball is thrown to someone, that person gives an opinion or answers a question. It is a useful way to involve more group members in the discussion in a non-threatening way.

2. Supporting. All good discussions occur in an atmosphere of openness. Allow your group members the freedom to express their points of view without punishment. Young people need to feel safe in sharing their opinions and answers. If kids are penalized through sarcasm, put-downs, or other forms of belittlement, your discussion will die. Examples of support include: "That's an interesting way of looking at the situation." "That's a good idea. Are there any other ideas?" "That's one way of looking at it." Examples of non-support include: "That's the wrong answer!" "Can anyone think of a better answer?" "That's stupid." "Use your brain."

3. Guiding. Many discussions fail because they are nothing more than bull sessions. For a good discussion to occur—one that produces healthy spiritual growth—it is imperative that you identify and work toward a goal or goals. Before beginning your discussion, complete the following three sentences to help structure your Zinger discussion toward a goal or goals:

   a. My goal(s) for the session is (are) ...
   b. For this goal to be reached, I must ...
   c. The things that might keep me from reaching my goal are ...

The discussion must be focused toward a particular goal or goals. Even when you move away from the main issue and focus on a tangential issue you are still working toward a goal. It is scattered dialogue that you want to avoid.

Another danger which parallels the bull session and will program your discussion for failure is the gripe session. Your young people will often focus an inordinate amount of their discussion time on the negative when they are telling their stories related to the Zinger situation. They will spend time gossiping about others, bad-mouthing their families, criticizing the church, or judging their schools. Some negative evaluations are inevitable and even necessary, but do attempt to keep the entire discussion from becoming a gripe session. Keep a balance between negative comments and positive solutions.

To keep the discussion moving, summarize the points made in the discussion, suggest moving in another direction, ask questions that redirect the discussion, or point out the time limit to your group.

4. Humor. Keep the discussion user-friendly. You will want to allow for jokes and fun during the discussion. As long as the laughter is not from put-downs, lighten the talk with humor.

5. Pausing. Silence makes many people uncomfortable. But silence is an important ingredient for a successful discussion. Pausing for ten to thirty seconds after a queston has been asked gives young people time to formulate their thoughts. Do not be afraid of silence. Use it to give kids time to reflect on what has been said and what has been asked.

6. Educating. Periodically, the group members will need to be given new information to help them grow. You will need to introduce new ideas, Scripture passages, or doctrinal teaching into the discussion. Keep it brief. There is not much room for lecture in the discussion method.

7. Probing. This is a tough skill to put into practice. It is the art of getting the group to dig deeper into an issue. Probing is done through questioning, clarifying, and summarizing. Probe with questions of the "how" and "why" type (see next section). When young people appear confused about a direction the discussion has taken, ask for clarity or clarify the meaning yourself. Examples of asking for clarity include: "What is another way of saying that?" "Apply that to your situation." "Could you be more specific about what you mean by that?" Another way to probe is by asking for a summary of the discussion. Simply ask a group member or two to summarize the discussion that has occurred so far. This will help your group see the flow and direction of the discussion so that you can take it to a deeper level.

8. Facilitating. A big mistake often made by leaders is taking sides in the discussion. Your role should be that of a facilitator. You want to stimulate discussion, which is best done by remaining neutral. You will get the opportunity to present your views during the closure of the discussion.

9. Monitoring. At times you may need to step out of your role as facilitator and intervene in the discussion. The following are three useful guidelines to help you decide when to intervene:

a. Gross errors of the truth that appear to be confusing many group members and that are being accepted as fact are a signal that you may need to interrupt the group and clarify the errors. Do this without lecturing or put-downs. See if you can get the young people to clarify the confused thinking without you doing so.

b. Continuous departure from the issue or issues being discussed should signal that the group does not understand the goal of the discussion and needs to be put back on track. You can ask the group to define the purpose of the discussion. Or there may be another, more pressing issue, that needs to be discussed. In that case, redirect the discussion to deal with this new issue.

c. Destructive behavior by members toward others in the group should signal the need to return to the Zinger ground rules.

The Right Questions for Discussion

Questioning is a technique that is best developed through experience. You will improve your question-asking ability the more you practice. There are, however, several tips we can offer you on the art of asking questions.

1. Try to warm up the group at the beginning of the discussion by getting eveyone to say something, even if it is only their name. Ask a yes or no question that everyone can respond to as a group.

2. Ask questions clearly enough for everyone to hear and understand.

3. When an individual responds to a question, have her or him talk to the group. Often young people will direct their answers to the leader. But this does not

facilitate good discussion. Redirect answers given to you as the leader to the whole group.

4. Begin with easy, non-threatening questions, then move to deeper, more probing questions.

5. Allow time for the group to debrief, debate, and process answers to questions rather than you doing so. After Mary answers a question, ask John what he thinks about Mary's response.

6. Gather several responses to one question before evaluating any of the responses.

7. Take a deeper look at responses to a question by probing for the whys and hows and basing them upon the whats.

8. Throw out the question to the group, then allow time (a few seconds) for the members to ponder the question before calling on someone specific to respond.

9. Prepare questions of your own. Do not feel locked into the questions provided in the Leader's Tips. Questions you prepare help you tailor the discussion to the needs of your group.

10. Do not answer all the questions yourself, even when questions are directed toward you. Redirect questions to the group.

11. Allow and encourage each group member to ask questions of the group. Do not get into a rut where the group expects you to ask all the questions.

12. Balance the distribution of questions between volunteers and non-volunteers. Do give group members the right to pass on answering a question.

13. If kids are not sharing, you may want to try breaking them into smaller groups.

14. Encourage but do not force kids to answer questions. If a young person cannot answer a question, you have two directions you can go. First, you can prompt the individual with hints and clues, or rephrase the question and ask the person to look at the issue in a different way. The second choice you have is to move to another group member or go to another question. If you choose to do this to keep the momentum and group interest, do so without embarrassing the individual.

15. Vary the types of questions you ask. There are several types of questions you can ask:

a. *Recall level questions* require your group to remember certain facts or information. "Who wrote the book of Romans?" or "What story from the Bible did we study last week?" are examples of recall level questions. Use these questions to take knowledge your group already has acquired and apply it to the present issue being discussed. If you are discussing parents you might ask the question, "When we talked about the family three weeks ago, what is one thing we learned about parents?"

b. *Comprehension level questions* measure understanding. They call on your group to translate, give in their own words, restate, paraphrase, illustrate, explain, or give an example of. "Could someone please paraphrase the Scripture that was read?" or "Could you restate that in your own words?" are examples of comprehension questions.

c. *Application level questions* push for transferring what was learned to new situations. They call on your group to respond, demonstrate, apply, relate, or generalize. "Now that we have learned that ... what are we going to do?" is an application question.

d. *Process level questions* ask your group to analyze and synthesize. They call on your group to compare and contrast, deduce, formulate, or develop. You may ask something like "Why do so many young people have trouble with lying?"

e. *Evaluation level questions* call for your group to pass judgment. They require your group to choose, decide, evaluate, judge, consider, select, argue, or appraise. An example would be "Is lying to parents right or wrong?"

16. Evaluate the questions you ask at the end of the session. Ask yourself if your questions stimulated thinking, created further questions, helped achieve the goal(s) of the session, and kept the interest of the group. This self-evaluation will help you advance your questioning skills.

How to Use a Zinger

Zingers are fun to do with kids. Zingers are flexible, easy to use, and require little preparation. Use the following four steps to make your Zinger discussions a success.

Zinger Preparation

Once you have chosen the Zinger or Zingers you wish to discuss, thoroughly read your selection. Read through the Leader's Tips following the Zinger. Each Leader's Tips contains:

1. Topic(s): This gives you an idea about the issue or issues addressed in the Zinger. Because a Zinger is a slice of life, a multitude of topics are addressed. You may choose to focus on an issue addressed in the Zinger but not listed under the topic.

2. Purpose: Briefly describes the intent of the Zinger discussion. You may wish to redesign the purpose to fit your group's needs.

3. Background Brief: Here you will find background information that briefs you concerning the topic.

4. Additional Questions: We have provided several questions that you can use to create dialogue and reflection. But do not feel limited to just these questions, and do not feel you need to ask every one of these questions. You will find yourself thinking of additional questions as you facilitate the discussion.

5. High Points: We have provided several brief points to help you with your concluding remarks.

6. Scripture: A passage is provided that your group can examine in relation to the Zinger topic. Incidentally, here's a suggestion. For those kids in your group who don't already have Bibles, I recommend Zondervan's *The Adventure Bible: The NIV Study Bible for Kids*. The NIV translation, of course, is easy for them to read and understand, and the study helps are great for nine-to-twelve-year-olds.

7. Additional Scripture: Biblical passages are given that you can refer to in supplementing the main passage of Scripture.

Talk yourself through the Zinger discussion adding or subtracting your own questions, high points, and Scripture. Make copies of the Zinger situation for each of the groups who will be discussing the Zinger. You can make copies for each young person in attendance if paper airplanes, spit wads, and paper snowball fights are not a problem for your group. We have given you permission to photocopy Zingers for your group. Please do not abuse this privilege by making copies for every children's ministry in your city.

Zinger Presentation

Introduce the topic of your Zinger discussion to the group or have one of the young people do so. Then briefly talk over the ground rules your group will use to guide the discussion.

Break into groups for the Zinger discussion and have someone read the Zinger situation. The larger your group, the more small groups you will want to divide into. We recommend groups of no more than five to ten. You can conduct a Zinger discussion with larger groups but understand that you will have many young people left out of the discussion. You may want to divide into same-sex groupings depending on the subject being discussed.

Zinger Guided Discussion

Once the Zinger has been read, the group should answer the questions at the end of the situation. Try to generate as many responses as possible. Out of this interaction your group members will begin to share their stories that are similar to the Zinger situation. It is important to foster this sharing time experience. You may want to say something like "Are there any of you who have had similar things happen to you or your friends? Could you share your story with the group?" You will want to maintain boundaries in the kinds of stories told. You do not want kids to glorify their sins or exaggerate the truth. You do want kids to feel free to talk about their own experiences, both good and bad.

In addition to the use of questions you will find brainstorming, 5 x 5s, and role plays valuable tools in guiding your group through a Zinger discussion.

Brainstorming is a simple technique that will help your group generate numerous opinions or solutions to a situation or problem. The leader begins the brainstorming session by stating the situation or problem and asking the group to consider as many ideas as possible. Here are several principles to guide your brainstorm sessions.

1. Quantity is more important than quality. List as many ideas as possible without passing judgment on any of them.
2. There should be no put-downs or criticism of anyone's ideas.
3. Encourage group members to piggyback or build upon each other's ideas to create new ideas.
4. Once all ideas have been collected the group can then go back and group their ideas together into themes, evaluate their ideas, and come to some sort of consensus opinion or solution.

The 5 x 5 is another simple yet effective technique that can help your young people generate ideas, choose positions on issues, or solve problems. Simply divide your group into groups of five people each. Tell each group they have five minutes to discuss the Zinger or question at hand and come up with a solution. One young person in each group should be selected to summarize and report his or her group's thinking to the large group.

Role playing is a technique you will find useful when you want to safely try out a skill like saying no to peer pressure in a true-to-life situation. Role plays involve real situations that your group members act out to practice how they would handle the situation. Role playing should only be used in groups who are well acquainted and trust each other. Here are four guiding principles to help you with Zinger role plays.

1. Use the Zinger situation or similar stories told to the group by the young people as your role-play situation.
2. Pick volunteers from your group to spontaneously act out the situations.
3. Ask the volunteer(s) who is practicing a new skill to try it out during the role play.

4. Debrief the role play with a large group discussion about what happened, including suggestions to the volunteer practicing the skill.

Zinger Wrap-up

Once all the issues have been identified and discussed, you need to bring the session to some sort of closure. Begin this process by introducing Scripture. Zinger discussions are somewhat different than many teaching activities for this age group in that they do not begin with Scripture. A Zinger discussion looks at the realities of life, then points to God and his Word as the answer. Once you have discussed the biblical passage(s), you have the opportunity to challenge the group with your concluding remarks. We have supplied you with several High Points to help you with your thoughts. As you consider your conclusion, ask yourself what one or two thoughts you will want your group members to leave the session remembering. End on an affirming high note full of love and hope. Be sure to let your young people know of your availability to talk with them individually after the session concerning issues that may be bothering them.

Choosing the Right Zinger for Your Group

The Zingers in this book were selected from the stories nine-to-twelve-year-old young people told us. We listened to the growing-up dilemmas of kids in both urban and suburban settings. We included minority, upper class to lower class, Christian and non-Christian kids in our sampling of stories. Just because a Zinger is found in this book does not mean it is appropriate for your group. All of the issues confronted in Zingers are true-to-life situations that face nine-to-twelve-year-olds—but maybe not *your* nine-to-twelve-year-olds. The following eight principles will help you choose the right Zinger to meet the needs of your group.

1. **Know the kids in your group well.** Children's workers need to be aware of the issues confronting their kids. Since the nine-to-twelve-year-old is confronted by issues new for adults, it is only natural that workers feel uncomfortable or are unaware of the issues. When you are choosing a Zinger it is imperative that you know the issues confronting the kids with whom you work. In spite of the homogenizing influence of television, there are still community and group differences that exist between kids. Some ten-year-olds are fairly involved in rock music while others are not. In some communities, nicotine and alcohol abuse are major problems for middle school youths, while in others these problems affect only older youths.

We have found that a simple yet effective

method for determining the appropriateness of a Zinger topic is through the use of a "circle share" group. To use this technique you will need to select four to six of your key young people. Explain to them that you need their feedback about several topics you are considering for discussion with the larger group. Hand out a copy of the index of this book to each of the young people sitting in your circle share group. Ask them to suggest topics from the index they believe the group needs to know more about. You can then take the time to read several of the Zingers and discuss their appropriateness for the larger group. Providing yourself with this kind of feedback will give you an idea about the kinds of Zingers your group needs to discuss.

2. Use wise judgment when choosing a Zinger. Some of the Zinger topics may be misunderstood or viewed as controversial. When you risk venturing into "uncharted discussion waters," you risk the criticism of others. Adults in your church, school, club, or wherever you are using Zingers may feel uncomfortable with you talking with young people about many of the Zinger issues found here.

There are times when you will find it better not to use a Zinger until you can educate potential critics about the necessity of discussing certain topics. Enlist the help of allies who can support you in educating adults about the new issues created by the growing-up-too-fast syndrome. Then you can proceed with a base of support rather than controversy.

3. Use Zingers as "Talk Treats." Like any other teaching technique, Zingers can be overused. We suggest that you use Zingers as a treat for your group. Pull them out when they supplement your Sunday school curriculum topic. Or use them as a special talk treat at one of your club meetings. Or if you are a classroom teacher, use them sporadically throughout the year to spark a good values discussion. You can also use two or three together in the same discussion.

We have offered you a wide variety of Zingers from which to choose. You do not need to use all of them. Keep them special. Flexible and adaptable, Zingers can be used in any children's group setting, from scout meetings to the Sunday school to the school classroom.

4. Do not use Zingers to contribute to the "growing-up-too-fast" syndrome. In our zeal to help children deal with the realities of their world we can sometimes contribute to the very things we are against. You must be careful not to create conflict and tension with issues for the sake of shocking kids. We need to present and deal with issues on the young people's developmental level. We need not become preoccupied with adult sexuality, the ugliness of divorce, death and suffering, adult themes of violence, and other such issues. However, we do need to focus on those issues

that confront our kids in their daily lives. In our striving to protect them from the realities of adult life we can leave them without the tools to deal with the realities of their lives. Nine-to-twelve-year-olds also need solid answers to help them cope with the realities of their world. Teenagers can deal with ambiguity, but preteens need concrete answers. Leaving them hanging or confused only serves to push them toward premature adulthood with its cynicism, mistrust, and loss of innocence.

5. Involve parents. It is absolutely necessary to include parents in any decisions you make regarding your choice of Zingers. Childrens' workers are partners with parents in teaching values and helping kids work through the dilemmas they face. One great way of keeping parents informed about your Zinger discussions is to provide parents with a copy of the Zingers you wish to use. You may also want to provide copies to other adults to whom you are accountable, such as Christian education committees, club leaders, or principals.

Another effective method for involving parents is to use the "circle share" method suggested for use with your kids. Parents can be a valuable resource in identifying the needs of this age group.

Finally, you can send a copy of the Zinger home with each of your kids with instructions to discuss them with their parents. This can be especially effective if parents know ahead of time and are prepared for a discussion time with their son or daughter.

6. Adjust Zingers to fit the needs of your group. When selecting a Zinger do not feel hemmed in by the stated purpose, topic, additional questions, or Scriptures. Each Zinger was written to reflect the realities of the world of today's preadolescent. This means that each Zinger contains a mixture of issues. Because Zingers can deal with a multitude of issues, you may choose to use a Zinger as a discussion starter for an issue other than the one(s) stated in the Leader's Tips. You may also find your group focusing on other issues during a Zinger discussion. There are times when you will want to refocus the discussion back to the main topic. However, there may be times where you will want to pursue the issue of interest if it involves a need your group wants to examine.

7. Lift the needs of your group to God in prayer. You may be surprised how God can reveal the needs of your group to you if you will only ask!

8. You are the final authority in choosing a Zinger. Keep in mind that you ultimately are the one who must decide what issues your group needs to discuss and what issues your group is not yet ready to handle. If you enter into a partnership with your young people and parents you will be able to use that authority wisely.

14

THE UNBELIEVABLE BREAK

This is the first summer Danny has ever made his own money. He even found the jobs himself, going around the neighborhood and asking people if they needed any odd jobs done around the house. So far this summer he has taken care of two different neighbors' homes while they were away on vacation, painted until his arms ached, cleaned out three garages, and held down four weekly lawn jobs.

Today he is weeding the garden of a close friend of his dad's, Mr. Nicholson. Squatting in a row of beans, his hands scratched and black with dirt, Danny dreams of the BB gun he will buy with the money he earns. Just then Mr. Nicholson comes out of the house. "Danny," he calls. "I'm going out to run errands. But I'm leaving the front door open so you can help yourself to a soda, okay?" Danny waves his "thank you" as Mr. Nicholson drives away.

The sun gets higher and hotter as it gets closer to noon. Danny wipes the sweat from his forehead. *Time for a break,* he thinks. *I'm thirsty.*

Danny pulls off his muddy shoes at the front door before going in. On his way to the kitchen he glimpses some magazines stacked on a coffee table. He looks closer. *Playboy* magazines! He hesitates, looks around, then picks up the top magazine and flips through it. Unbelievable! *This might be the longest break time in the history of yard work,* he thinks as he settles himself into a chair, magazine in hand.

How would you feel if you were Danny?

How should Danny handle this situation?

GROUP:_____

DATE USED:_____

The Unbelievable Break Leader's Tips

Topic: Pornography
Purpose: To help kids see that pornography is wrong and harmful.
Background Brief:

These days pornography is ubiquitous. Children used to be protected from the evils of porn; at best, they had to sneak looks at *National Geographic* magazines, for a glimpse of nudity. Today, however, children have easier access to pornography. Many mall bookstores, libraries, and convenience stores openly display porn magazines. Cable, off-color music videos, and rental movies transform televisions into porn machines.

Children are curious by nature. When their need for a healthy sex education is not met, many children satisfy their need to know by turning to pornography. Obviously, this is not the sex education that God intended. Pornography gives children misleading information and a distorted, inaccurate presentation of sexuality.

Kids will not innately resist the temptation of pornography, especially since they live in a culture actively promoting it. Your group members are not buying porn magazines or renting X-rated videos, but they are being exposed to sexually perverted materials. Perhaps they have peeked at a pornographic magazine at the mall or a friend's house. Or perhaps they have watched X-rated movies on the VCR.

After reading and talking about this Zinger, use the experiences of your kids to role-play reactions to pornography. This is a very sensitive issue, so handle it carefully. Perhaps you will want to demonstrate how to say no to pornography through a role-play with other adults.

Additional Questions:

1. What is pornography?
2. Why does pornography make God angry?
3. Would you be tempted to look at the *Playboy* magazines if you were Danny?
4. Why do you think Mr. Nicholson looks at *Playboy*?
5. If this really happened to you, would you tell your parents? Should you?

High Points:

1. Curiosity about pornography is normal.
2. God created our bodies to be special.
3. Pornography uses people's bodies in a wrong way.
4. Pornography perverts God's plan for healthy relationships.
5. Pornography makes God angry.

Scripture: Luke 11:33-36

Ask the group to give examples of times they tried to do something outside (like one of their chores) when it was getting dark. Use the groups' stories to illustrate the point that light makes it easier to do something correctly. Or, if you are in a room that can be darkened, turn the lights out and have the group perform a safe task that is difficult to do in the dark, like playing a game or looking up a passage of Scripture. With the lights back on, talk with the group about darkness and how it makes simple tasks more difficult.

In Luke 11 Jesus was trying to teach (metaphorically) that when our lives are spiritually darkened, it becomes more difficult to do what is right. Christ points out that there is a choice to be made: will we fill ourselves with light so that we can more easily do what is right, or will we fill ourselves with darkness so that it becomes more difficult to do what is right?

Addtional Scripture:

Genesis 6:5-7
Psalm 19:14
1 Peter 2:11

AIDS ALERT

Jeff is a seventh grader at Johnson Middle School. Recently there was a big battle over AIDS education in the school. Parents came out in droves to talk about the issue. Like most other students, Jeff thinks AIDS education is a big joke. When a newspaper reporter interviewed him about the AIDS education class, this is what he said:

"Adults act like we are all going to go out and get AIDS. Like I'm sure someone in middle school is going to get AIDS! Do they think we are all shooting drugs or having sex with prostitutes or homosexuals? The PTA had a big meeting to discuss how they would teach us about AIDS. The TV news was here for the meeting and everything. It took forever. Anyway, I was in that AIDS education class yesterday, and it was no big deal. I still don't see why people are making such a fuss about AIDS. I think it's all pretty stupid."

How would you feel if you were Jeff?

How should Jeff handle this situation?

Aids Alert Leader's Tips

Topic: AIDS education

Purpose: To help young people process information they are receiving about AIDS (Acquired Immune Deficiency Syndrome).

Background Brief:

Even though AIDS may seem a very sensitive topic to cover at such a young age, many elementary and middle schools now require AIDS education as a part of their curriculum. If the young people involved in your ministry are receiving such education at school, processing the information taught them can be crucial. Much secular sex education focuses upon the crisis aspect of sex—the crisis of sexually transmitted diseases, pregnancy, homosexuality, birth control, and sexual dysfunctions. The media focus is no different with its preoccupation with rape, molestation, AIDS, prostitution, etc.

This distorted, crisis-oriented view of sex can both scare and anesthetize young people to the beauty and wonder of our God-created sexuality.

This Zinger will help your young people talk about their concerns and questions regarding AIDS. Before you use this Zinger, however, you will need to educate yourself regarding the AIDS issue. You will also need to contact the schools your young people attend to find out what is being taught. Most schools encourage reviews of their curriculum by parents and interested adults. If you can't visit all the schools your young people attend, you can at least check out with a phone call what is happening at the schools.

It is best to use this Zinger in the context of a broader, more comprehensive biblical sex education curriculum, which ideally should include the parents. If you use the Zinger as a single teaching activity, be sure to present it in the context of a larger picture of God-created sex. By focusing simply on the AIDS epidemic, you can make the same mistake as the secular sex educator of focusing only on the crisis aspects of sex.

Leading a discussion on AIDS may initially be difficult because young people feel uncomfortable talking about sexual issues, especially with adults. To facilitate the discussion set ground rules such as: no put-downs, no such thing as a dumb question, confidentiality. If young people are able to ask questions, they are old enough to get honest answers. Don't make the mistake of believing the myth that talking about sex will encourage it. This just is not true. Young people need accurate information and biblical values presented to them to help them make future godly choices. Ignorance and secrets have never contributed to healthy sexual development.

Additional Questions:

1. What have you learned about AIDS at your school?
2. What do you know about AIDS?
3. Why are many parents scared and concerned because of AIDS?
4. Could someone your age get AIDS?
5. What might God think of the AIDS epidemic?

High Points:

1. AIDS is not a punishment from God on bad, sinful people. If this were true, everyone would be sick in the hospital, for we are all sinners.
2. We need to show Christian love and compassion to people sick with AIDS.
3. Touching someone with AIDS is safe.
4. Sex was created by God as a beautiful expression of love between a married couple.
5. Abstinence or married sex give the best protection against infection from AIDS.

Scripture: Luke 5:12-13

The church's reaction to the AIDS epidemic has ranged from compassion to condemnation of homosexuals and I.V. drug users. Spiritually, as followers of Christ, how should we respond to AIDS? Unfortunately, most discussions of AIDS simply focus on how to avoid infection. But Christians need to look beyond the secular advice for safe sex and clean needles to confront the AIDS sufferers themselves.

Luke 5 will help you emphasize to your young people God's love for the AIDS-infected person. A similar disease afflicted people in the days of Jesus. Like AIDS, leprosy had no cure. People with leprosy were considered "untouchables" and were treated as outcasts. People in Bible times thought leprosy was highly contagious, so they would not touch an infected leper. However, Jesus reached out with healing compassion to physically touch the leper.

Christ offers Christians a model for how to treat those afflicted with the terrible AIDS virus. Even though many people see AIDS-infected individuals as "untouchables," Jesus wishes Christians to reach out to them with love.

Additional Scripture:

Luke 4:27   Romans 6:23   Ephesians 5:1-3

18

A TOUCHY SITUATION

Sarah slams her locker and runs down the hall. If she doesn't hurry, she'll miss her bus. Walking home isn't so bad, but she wants to get home quickly to tell her mom about the A she received on her math test.

The usual crowd is waiting for the bus. Sarah goes to the end of the line hoping she'll get a good seat. The bright yellow bus pulls into the lot and she climbs aboard, scanning the crowded bus for an empty seat.

There! Sarah spots an empty seat. And it's next to Andy Simms, the cutest boy in school. All the girls want to get to know him.

"Now's my chance!" Sarah thinks. Smiling, she asks Andy if she can sit next to him. Andy grins back, his brown eyes gleaming, and moves his legs so Sarah can sit by the window. He slings his arm casually over the back of the seat.

When the bus starts up Sarah feels Andy's arms drop around her shoulder. She's thrilled. There they sit, like boyfriend-girlfriend, Andy's hand on her shoulder. *Andy must really like me!* Sarah thinks.

But before she knows what is happening, Andy's hand slips down the side of her arm and touches her breast. She looks at him, but he just puts his hand back on her shoulder and smiles at her as if nothing has happened.

Sarah feels cold and sick inside. *What do I do?* she wonders. All her happiness has turned to confusion.

How would you feel if you were Sarah?

How should Sarah handle this situation?

SAFETY EXIT ⇨

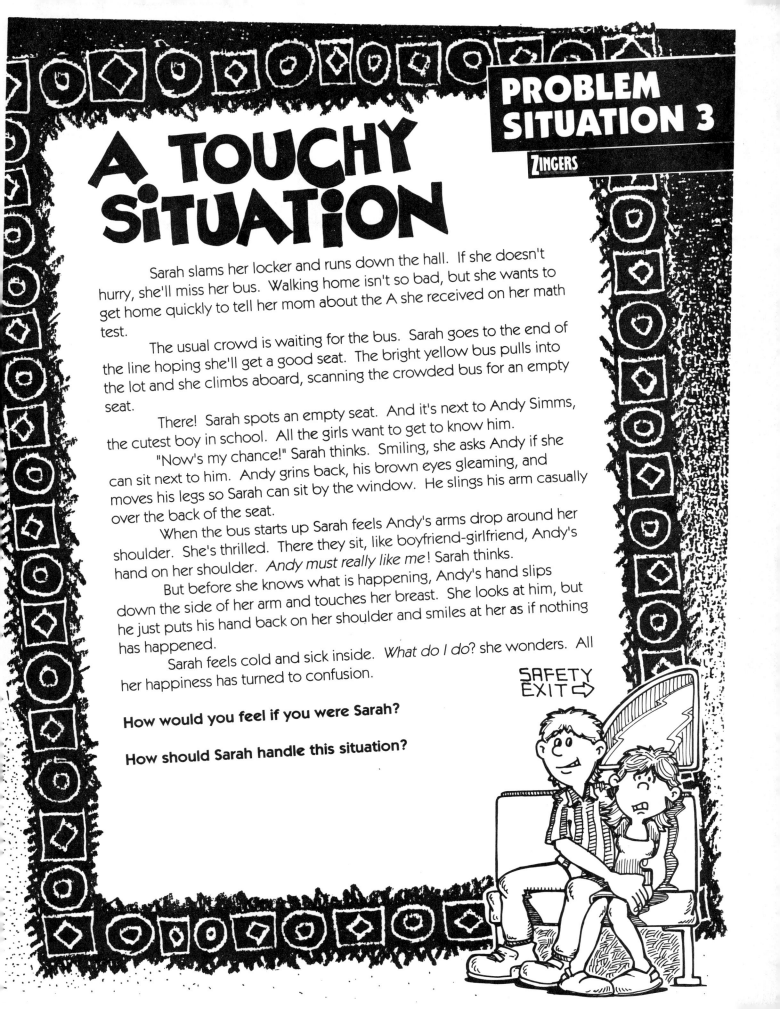

GROUP:_____
DATE USED:_____

ZINGERS

A Touchy Situation Leader's Tips

Topic: Sexual exploitation

Purpose: To help young people process the sexual confusion they face during the formative pre-adolescent years.

Background Brief:

There will be times during pre-adolescent years when young people are confronted with confusing sexual messages. They may hear a bizarre sexual story from a classmate, receive an obscene phone call, become friends with a sexual abuse victim, or even experience some form of sexual exploitation themselves.

Touch is especially confusing for this age group. Young people at this age begin to experience touching outside their families: hugs from friends, kisses, back rubs, wrestling, etc. Some of this touch is very caring and healthy. Yet much of it is new and confusing: an unexpected hug, a pat on the bottom, a kiss from the opposite sex, kissing games, holding hands. Or, as in the case presented in this Zinger, a boy touching a girl's breast.

Often there is a "No Talk" rule in church education surrounding sex. Consequently, young people seek out answers from their peers, pornography, and the media. This Zinger can help you break the "No Talk" rule.

This Zinger is best used in the context of a broader, more comprehensive biblical sex education curriculum that includes parental participation. If it is used as a single teaching activity, young people may ask questions and relate stories about a broad range of sexual topics. It will be up to you to keep the discussion focused or to move in a new direction.

This topic, sexual exploitation, is processed best when boys and girls are separated. Same-sex groupings seem to ease the tension that exists when this topic is discussed in mixed company. However, it can be useful to have a male and female adult leader in each same-sexed group to provide both perspectives.

Leading a discussion on this topic may initially be difficult, because young people feel uncomfortable talking about sexual issues, especially with adults. To facilitate the discussion, set ground rules such as: no put-downs, no such thing as a dumb question, confidentiality. If young people are able to ask a question, they are old enough to get an honest answer. Don't make the mistake of believing the myth that talking about sex will encourage it. This just is not true. Kids need accurate information and biblical values presented to them to help them make future godly choices. Ignorance and secrets have never contributed to healthy sexual development.

Additional Questions:

1. Has this kind of thing ever happened to anyone you know?
2. How involved should a boy and girl your age become?
3. What do you usually do when you are confused about a situation?
4. How can these kinds of situations be avoided?
5. Whose fault was this—Sarah's or Andy's? (Author's note: This was clearly Andy's fault.)

High Points

1. Young people need to talk with their parents or a trusted Christian adult about confusing sexual incidents they hear from friends, view in the media, or experience.
2. Talking with a parent or other trustworthy adult about one's confusion can help a person make sense of a feeling or event.
3. God intended experiences like holding hands, hugging, or kissing the opposite sex to be good. However, these eperiences can also be bad and exploitive.
4. When someone does or wants to do something to you that is confusing, you have the right to say no. God created your body for you, not someone else.

Scripture: Proverbs 1:7-9

Here, in this passage of Scripture, Solomon advises young people not to be know-it-alls. Rather, they should seek wisdom for living from the Lord. In addition, Solomon tells young people to be open to the advice and wisdom of parents or other Christian adults. God is the only know-it-all, but adults can help people who are struggling and confused. Young people need to discover that they can learn from the experience of others.

Additional Scripture:

Proverbs 6:20-24
Proverbs 9:10

SATURDAY NIGHT SUNDAY MORNING

It's Thursday night, and Margarita and Veronica are talking on the phone, planning a trip to the mall on Saturday. Veronica has to buy a new pair of jeans, and she wants Margarita's advice. They are trying to decide what time to go.

"Hey, Margarita, why don't we go later, and then you can spend the night?" Veronica suggests.

"Let me ask my mom," Margarita replies.

Margarita puts down the phone, but she doesn't call her mother. She knows already that her mom will say no. Her mother never lets her spend Saturday night away from home because her family always goes to church together early on Sunday morning. Margarita likes going to church with her family. But sometimes it is embarrasing to explain.

Margarita sighs deeply and picks up the receiver. "Oh, Veronica," she says, "I can't spend the night."

She decides to tell the truth. "My mom won't let me because of church tomorrow morning."

"Church!" Veronica sounds angry. "You go to church? Nobody goes to church. How are you going to stay popular if you go to church? Just tell your mom you don't want to go."

How would you feel if you were Margarita?

How should Margarita handle this situation?

GROUP:_____
DATE USED:_____

Saturday Night, Sunday Morning
Leader's Tips

Topic: Christianity, church, popularity
Purpose: To help young people talk about the tension that exists between friendships and Christian beliefs.

Background Brief:
Children at this age begin to compare their family religious beliefs to those of their friends. They may even make fun of others who do not believe the way they do.

Preadolescents also have strong desires to form personal relationships. Friendships and popularity, traditionally considered major adolescent issues, have now been pushed down into the upper elementary grades. Wearing the right clothes, saying the right things, being "cool"— all are important to this age group.

At this age a "check-it-out-for-oneself" attitude develops, and the preadolescent begins to test out family-taught values. This attitude combined with the need for relationships and popularity can place Christian beliefs in tension with friendship needs. Young people may begin to test out what they believe to see if it is "cool" or acceptable with their peers.

Use this Zinger to give your group a chance to talk about the tension that often exists between church/Christianity and popularity.

Additional Questions:
1. What might you say to Veronica?
2. Has church ever interfered with your social life?
3. How do your friends that do not go to church affect your attitude towards church?
4. What about church do you like the most? The least?
5. What would happen if you invited your friends to church?
6. Why is church attendance important?

High Points:
1. Church is a family of Christians who get together to worship God, who love and serve each other, and who reach out to the world as a testimony for Christ.
2. God wants you to have friends.
3. You, as a Christian, can reach out with love to your friends.
4. Church is a place where you can talk about the frustrations you have with friends and popularity.

Scripture: Hebrews 10:22-25
This Scripture speaks to Christians about the opportunities we have to pray to God, to grow in faith, to encourage each other, and to worshp God. Those who miss attending church, the gathering of the saints together, lose out on the opportunity to receive encouragement and strength from other Christians.

Additional Scripture:
1 Corinthians 12:12-13
Ephesians 3:14-19
1 Thessalonians 5:11

PARANOID PARENTS

Chris and Peter are sitting at the lunch table. They just got out of science class, where they discussed drugs. They're still talking about the class.

"Man, my parents are paranoid," Chris complains. "They're so afraid I'm going to do drugs." He stirs the stew on his plate and makes a face.

His mouth full, Peter says, "So what's their problem?"

Chris shrugs. "I don't know. I guess they think I'll get influenced by the wrong crowd. Every time I want to change my hairstyle or the way I dress they go crazy. And when my swim team had a party, they volunteered to be chaperones—to spy on me, I bet." He swallows some milk. "I told them I'll never do drugs, but they won't believe me." Chris looks over at Peter. "How are your parents?" he asks.

"Mine are paranoid too," Peter says. "Especially after what happened last week."

"What?"

"A guy was shot a couple blocks from our house—because of drugs."

"Wow," Chris says.

Peter nods. "Yeah, and boy, did I ever get the lecture about drugs. I see what you mean. I wish our parents would just stay off our backs."

How would you feel if you were Chris and Peter?

How should Chris and Peter handle this problem?

GROUP:_____

DATE USED:_____

Paranoid Parents Leader's Tips

Topics: Alcohol, drugs, parents

Purpose: To help young people understand their parents' worries regarding alcohol and drug abuse.

Background Brief:

What parent today does not worry about alcohol and drug abuse by their preadolescent or adolescent child? The alcohol and drug problem has even reached its ugliness down to children. Young people in this age group increasingly experiment with alcohol, nicotine, and inhalants. Kids have access to alcohol because so many parents are working. The after-school hours leave youngsters free to experiment with what is in the refrigerator (beer, wine coolers) and the liquor cabinet (harder stuff). Also, kids begin to experiment with smoking and chewing at this age.

A very scary trend that affects a number of young people at this age is the use of inhalants like gasoline, nail polish, glue, liquid paper, etc. Sniffing is quite common and problematic among upper elementary school and middle school kids.

Also, at this age, young people begin to see parental involvement in their lives as an interference. Unfortunately, many parents get involved with their children only when there are problems. Kids begin to see their parents' concern about legitimate issues as obtrusive and "turn off" to their parents good intentions.

Give your group members a chance to discuss why their parents worry so much about them. Brainstorm some parental concerns about alcohol and drugs. Ask the group if alcohol and drug use might also be issues in their lives, as well as issues that their parents need to be concerned about.

Additional Questions:

1. How many of you know or have parents like Chris's and Peter's?
2. Why do you think parents worry so much about alcohol and drugs?
3. How can you help calm your parents' fears?
4. How can you show your parents you can be trusted?

High Points:

1. It is normal for parents to worry about their kids. Parents have a lot to worry about in today's world.
2. Spending time talking with your parents will help them worry less.
3. Parental trust is something that you earn.
4. God gave your parents the responsibility to raise you.
5. If you have friends who are experimenting with smoking, drinking, or drugs, your parents will have a more difficult time believing you can make mature decisions.
6. If you have friends who drink, smoke, or do drugs, you will be more likely to do the same.

Scripture: Proverbs 4:1-6

Solomon here tells the reader how his father David encouraged him to seek wisdom. (Perhaps this is why Solomon asked God to bless him with wisdom above all other things.) This passage illustrates how wisdom can be passed from a parent to a child. Parents want their children to have wisdom and develop good discernment and judgment skills, especially for dealing with the dangers of alcohol and drugs. Use this passage of Scripture to emphasize that kids need to listen to the wisdom of their parents. And point out the promise given in this passage to young people who heed the wisdom of their parents—protection and a long life.

Additional Scripture:

Ephesians 6:1-3
Colossians 3:20

WAVING COLOR

Lemont lives in a tough part of town. If the stores aren't closed and boarded up, they have bars in front of their windows. The only color besides gray cement comes from the spray-painted graffiti on the walls and sidewalks. There are at least four gangs around: the Fifth Street gang, the Roaches, the Dragonmen, and the Coppers.

Lemont doesn't want to be a gang member, but he doesn't have much choice. Kids younger than he is have already joined the Fifth Street gang. It's the only way to get respect—and protection too. Recently the other gangs have been hassling Lemont on the school playground. Maybe if he joins the Fifth Street gang, the other gangs will leave him alone.

Now Lemont's best friend Tyrone is trying to get Lemont to join. "What's the big deal, man?" he says. "Fifth Streeters don't do nothing bad. They just save your skin when you need them."

Everybody seems to belong to a gang. Lemont wants to be accepted and protected too. Should he become a Fifth Streeter?

How would you feel if you were Lemont?

How should Lemont handle this situation?

Waving Color Leader's Tips

Topic: Gangs

Purpose: To help young people recognize the effects of gang involvement in their lives, and to give them an opportunity to explore alternatives to gang involvement.

Background Brief:

It seems that today's news, whether in the paper, a magazine, or the television, always includes a story about gangs. The story is rarely a happy one. Gangs, with their drugs and violence, are on the rise. Gang-related music, clothing, and slang are making their way into the youth culture at large. The romanticized gangs of the 1950's "Westside Story" no longer exist. Today, hard-core gangs' craziness is the norm.

If gang activity affects your ministry, you can use this Zinger to approach the subject of gang involvement with your group. The preadolescent is quite often pressured into gang activity. Because movies and newscasts glamorize gang activity, many young people pretend to be involved in gangs.

Allow your group the opportunity to discuss gang activity in their neighborhoods. Most likely some member or members of the group will sensationalize gang-related behavior, slang, dress, or music. It is best to process this sensationalism with the group without putting anyone down. If you can involve a Christian adult who is a former gang member in the discussion, do so. Use this person as well as group members to help you propose alternatives to gang involvement.

Additional Questions:

1. Why do people join gangs?
2. What gangs are in our neighborhood/community?
3. What might keep someone from joining a gang?
4. What happens to young people who join gangs?

High Points:

1. Gang involvement can only lead to disaster.
2. God created people to need a group for love, protection, fellowship, and encouragement. God has given Christians the church and the family to meet those needs.
3. Resisting gang involvement can be difficult.
4. God can give you the strength to be your own person.

Scripture: Proverbs 1:10-19

Here Solomon warns of the consequences of choosing gang involvement. Initially, the sins of gang activity look attractive. A young person seems to get "something for nothing." But, as this passage points out, the sin of gang involvement only leads to further sin and ultimate death. Solomon clearly tells anyone tempted to join a gang to run from the temptation. The short-term gains of being part of a gang may look good, but the long-term consequences are not worth it.

Additional Scripture:

Psalm 1
Proverbs 13:20
1 Corinthians 10:13
1 Corinthians 15:33

WATCHING MUSIC

Mark is arguing with his mother. She just came home and found him watching music videos on cable television–against her orders.

"But Mom," Mark says, "I'm the only kid in the whole world who doesn't watch MTV! Everyone else gets to."

"The answer is still *no*," his mother says firmly. "We don't like the values they show. We want the best for you, and music videos aren't the best."

Mark can tell by his mom's tone of voice that the subject is closed. He stomps out of the house. *No use trying to make her understand, he thinks. She's never even seen a music video, so how does she know they're so bad?*

Wandering down the street, he decides to see if Jeff is home. Jeff has cool parents. Sometimes Jeff's mom and dad even watch music videos with Jeff.

Why can't my parents be more like Jeff's? Mark wonders as he knocks at Jeff's front door. He hears Jeff coming to the door, and through the window can see the flickering TV. *Oh well, I can always watch videos here,* he thinks, smiling to himself.

How would you feel if you were Mark?

How should Mark have handled this situation?

How would you feel if you were Mark's mother?

How should Mark's mother handle this situation?

Watching Music Leader's Tips

Topic: Honesty, music videos, parents, rock music
Purpose: To give young people the opportunity to discuss the impact of music videos on their lives.
Background Brief:
Since the early '80s, the popularity of music videos has soared. Rock-'n-roll of the '50s, '60s, and '70s pales in comparison to the visual death, destruction, and exploitive sex portrayed in some of today's music videos. The visual promotion of free sex, drug abuse, bad language, the occult and the demonic, idolatry, anti-authority, and rebellion concern many parents.

At the same time, however, many of today's music videos promote positive values of justice, love, and compassion. Any discussion of music videos needs to be balanced and kept in perspective. Labeling all music videos as bad (or good) does little to help young people develop critical listening and viewing skills.

Most, if not all, of your group members have watched rock music videos. In fact, it is at this age, not adolescence, that young people establish listening and viewing patterns. Use this opportunity to dialogue with your group about the need to be selective in what they listen to and watch.

Additional Questions:
1. If you were Mark's parents and you caught him watching music videos against your orders, what would you do?
2. How can watching music videos hurt you? Help you?
3. Would you turn off a video that was bad?
4. How can you tell the difference between a good music video and a bad one?

High Points:
1. Music videos can be good as well as bad.
2. Some music videos go against Christian values.
3. God wants you to use your common sense and good judgment when choosing what type of music videos to watch.
If you are watching a video that is bad, turn it off.

Scripture: Philippians 4:8
What people put into their minds is what comes out in attitudes and actions. When people view videos with sinful themes, then sin will be result. The apostle Paul encourages Christians in this passage to examine what they put into their minds.

Additional Scripture:
Luke 6:48
Ephesians 5:19-20

PLAY DUMB

Derek watched as his little brother Chad got spanked for the third time that week. He thought Chad was pretty dumb for getting into trouble all the time.

Derek hardly ever got into trouble. He'd developed a system. Whenever he got caught, he'd pretend he didn't know what was going on. Then, if his parents got mad, he'd tell them what had happened, but he'd say as little as possible. He thought it was a great plan because he didn't have to lie, and it worked almost every time.

"I'd better give Chad some coaching," he muttered to himself. "He talks too much. I've got to teach him to shut up and play dumb."

Is what Derek does right or wrong?

Why?

GROUP:_____

DATE USED:_____

Play Dumb Leader's Tips

Topics: Deceit, parents.

Purpose: To help young people understand the importance of being honest with their parents.

Background Brief:

Preadolescence is a time of transition between childhood and adolescence. One aspect of this transition is a change in the relationship young people have with their parents. Both the child and the parent must move from a parent/child to a parent/adolescent relationship. The preadolescent forces the parent/child relationship to change whether or not the parent is comfortable with the change. At this age, young people want to feel more grown up. Their abilities and skills are increasing, their interest in more mature things expands, and their desire for independence grows. Often, the preadolescent seeks more independence than a parent is ready to allow. In order to gain independence, the young person may resort to avoiding or manipulating parents, as does Derek in this Zinger.

Young people need to realize that this period of change is as hard on their parents as it is on them. It is a scary time for parents as they watch their child take on the trappings of adolescence.

Young people want to feel that their parents trust them. They must learn that trust is earned and is not a benefit of age. Deceit leads to mistrust. If young people decide to choose Derek's method of dealing with their parents, then they must be ready to face the consequences.

Additional Questions:

1. Is Derek lying by what he does?
2. How will Derek's behavior affect his relationship with his parents?
3. Why is it important to take responsibility for your behavior?
4. What things do you do to deceive your parents?
5. How honest does God want you to be with your parents?

High Points:

1. Growing up is as confusing to parents as it is to young people.
2. With each birthday, you will want and need more independence.
3. Demonstrate your maturity in handling more independence with behaviors that foster trust in your parents.
4. When you are wrong, show your maturity by accepting the discipline your parents give you.

Scripture: Psalm 139:23-24

In this passage David asks God to search his life for deceitful ways. Young people who want a better relationship with their parents can ask God to point out when they have wronged their parents.

Additional Scripture:

Ephesians 6:1-4
Hebrews 12:5-11

THE PRESENT

Leah had been baby-sitting for weeks to earn money for her brother's birthday present. Aaron really wanted a special model car he had seen at the craft and hobby shop in the mall. She now had enough money to purchase the model plus a little extra to spend on herself.

Leah made sure she had money for the bus and then went to tell her mother she was leaving. Her mom said she was really proud of her hard work as she hugged Leah good-bye.

Leah hopped off the bus and strolled into the mall. On the way to the hobby shop she passed her favorite store.

Then she saw it—the sweater she had admired in *Seventeen*. It was a soft green, *her* color, and was embroidered with tiny yellow flowers.

She checked the price. Then she checked the sizes. Only one sweater was left in her size.

"I've got to have this sweater!" she whispered to herself. "I'll look great in it."

Leah checked her money. She had enough for the sweater and some left over for a present for her brother. She couldn't get him the model, but at least she would get him something.

She tried the sweater on. Sure enough, it looked wonderful on her. Leah took the sweater to the cashier and paid for it. Then she left for the hobby shop to find something she could afford for Aaron's birthday present.

Was what Leah did right or wrong?

Why?

The Present Leader's Tips

Topics: Selfishness, materialism

Purpose: To help young people reflect on materialism in their own lives.

Background Brief:

Americans are bombarded with the message that "things" give life meaning and purpose. Television overwhelms its viewers with a materialistic philosophy of life. The American dream of having lots of stuff diverts the attention of many adults from what is really important in life: Jesus Christ, family, friends, and service to others. Ask elderly individuals about how they would relive their lives and you can be certain that acquiring more things would not be a part of their plans. Yet getting lots of "stuff" seems to be the game plan of many.

This materialistic emphasis has not by-passed young people. What adults have bought as a way of life has not been lost on children. Young people have been given the message that things make life meaningful, and so they too love to gather stuff. Use this Zinger to talk about the emphasis the American culture places on materialism. Give young people the time to reflect on their own selfishness and materialism. Challenge them to consider ways they can move away from a materialistic lifestyle.

Additional Questions:

1. Do you think Leah intended to buy her brother the model car for his birthday?
2. Why do you think Leah went into her favorite store?
3. Is Leah a bad person?
4. How will Leah's mom feel now?
5. Why do we sometimes talk ourselves into doing things that we know are not right?

High Points:

1. You are tempted by material things every day.
2. Material things are not what make people happy, although things can appear to do so.
3. Materialism can get us to take our eyes off what is important—Jesus Christ.
4. God desires that Christians live simply so they can share what they have with others.

Scripture: Luke 12:16-21

Paraphrase this story for your group to illustrate the futility of getting lots of "stuff." A Christian's security is not in material things, nor does his or her purpose in life come from things. Rather, a Christian's life revolves around the person of Jesus Christ.

Additional Scripture:

Mark 8:34-36

Mark 10:17-31

1 John 3:17-18

FOUR EYES

Margie took the glasses out of the case, then went over to the mirror and put them on. She stared at herself for a long moment. She pulled a face. "I won't wear them," Margie muttered, tearing the glasses from her face. "They make me look gross. Kids will call me 'Four Eyes' and laugh at me—I just know they will."

Margie was miserable. She and her mom had just picked up her new glasses. She did not want them, but it was getting harder and harder for her to see the chalkboard at school. Margie wanted to get some designer frames or at least a cool color, but her mom said they should get something more practical until she was older. So here she was stuck with these boring brown plastic frames.

'Practical' must be another word for gross," Margie grumbled. She shoved the glasses back in their case and flopped onto her bed.

"I won't wear them," she said.

Just then her mother came in. She saw Margie's sour face. "You don't like your glasses, do you, honey?" she said.

Margie shook her head angrily and refused to speak.

"You'll get used to them, Margie," her mother said. "If you don't wear them, your vision will just get worse." She got up to leave, and at the door she said, "Margie, you're still the same pretty girl you were before. Glasses don't change that."

A lot she knows, thought Margie. *I look like a geek. I don't care if I can't see. I may wear glasses at home when Mom's around, but I'll never wear them at school.*

Is Margie right or wrong?

Why?

Is Margie's mother right or wrong?

Why?

Four Eyes Leader's Tips

Topics: Personal appearance, self-esteem
Purpose: To help young people handle the pressures related to their personal appearance.
Background Brief:

"Four Eyes," "Pizza Face," "Amazon," "Thunder Thighs," "Metal Mouth." You may remember a name you were called when young. And you can still feel the pain when you hear the name whispered in your mind. Young people are no different today when it comes to physical appearance than when you were growing up. In fact, the pressure today to conform to a certain look can be even more intense.

One reason young people are preoccupied with looks during preadolescence is physical. Children begin their growth spurts during this time, not in their adolescence as most adults think. Girls begin a rapid growth period at ten on the average, peaking at age twelve. Boys begin theirs a year to a year and a half behind girls and peak at about the age of 14. The physical changes that occur during preadolescence places tremendous pressure on the young person to adjust to a growing body.

The media places additional pressure on the preadolescent through its images of what it means to grow up. Consequently, young people worry about makeup, muscles, and wearing the right brand names. They do, however, come by this preoccupation with physical appearance honestly, since many of their baby-boomer parents are worried about the same things. Remember that the baby-boom generation created an America preoccupied with looking good and looking young.

Discussing this Zinger can help your group members share their feelings about personal appearance and the pressure to look good. Any put-downs during the discussion need to be processed immediately. When young people risk sharing their concerns, they need to know they can find Christian love and support, not the hurt they sometimes receive at school or elsewhere.

Do not make the mistake of telling your group that outward appearance is not important or what others say about appearance does not matter. It does matter!

Additional Questions:
1. Why do young people feel so uncomfortable when they look different?
2. Why do young people make fun of other kids who look different?
3. Why does it matter so much what other young people think of you?
4. How does Christ want you to treat young people who are different?

High Points:
1. God is not against your looking your best.
2. Preoccupation with looks can trick you into thinking that outer beauty is all there is.
3. God wants you to focus on inner character more than outward appearance.
4. True beauty really is more than skin deep.

Scripture: 1 Samuel 16:7
Tell your group the story of the prophet Samuel seeking a new king for Israel to replace Saul. God commands Samuel to anoint one of the sons of Jesse as the new king. Since King Saul was tall and handsome, Samuel may have been looking for someone similar as the new king. So God warned Samuel not to judge on the basis of physical attractiveness. God tells us that people may focus on outward appearance, but he is more concerned about what is inside.

Additional Scripture:
Luke 16:15
Romans 8:35-39
1 Peter 3:3-5

TROOPING OUT

It was Tuesday night: scout night. Grant stood in front of his closet, staring at his blue and gray uniform and wondering if he wanted to put it on.

Grant had been involved in scouting for as long as he could remember. He loved studying nature and learning survival skills. He liked his fellow scouts as well as the scout leader. His parents had both been involved with his troop and seemed to enjoy it as much as he did.

But lately Grant had been feeling uncomfortable. Some of his friends weren't scouts, and they thought Grant was weird for being one. Last Saturday when he was at the Scout-a-Rama at the mall, one of his friends saw him in his uniform and called him a dweeb.

Grant tried to talk with his dad about how embarrassed he felt, but his dad didn't seem to understand. All he said was, "Don't let what other people say bother you."

Reluctantly, Grant pulled the uniform out of the closet and put it on. He hoped no one would call while he was gone, especially not Jason or Chris. They really thought scouting was for nerds. Maybe he would just tell his mother not to tell anyone who called that he was at a scout meeting.

Was Grant right or wrong?

Why?

GROUP:_____

DATE USED:_____

Trooping Out Leader's Tips

Topics: Conformity, lying

Purpose: To help young people develop ways of dealing with situations when they feel different from others.

Background Brief:

What are some things that make you feel different? No one likes to feel different. There is security in being a part of a group. Look at your friends: You share similar tastes, interests, jobs, or ministries. Young people have an even greater need to feel a part of the group, to look just enough like everyone else to be a part of the crowd.

Friends become more important to the preadolescent than they were during childhood. The nine to eleven year old is focused on same-sex friendships, with parents still exerting a strong influence. However, at the end of this age period, the young person begins to become interested in the opposite sex, friendship clusters become even more important, and parental influence begins to decline somewhat. The eleven- to thirteen-year-old is usually more willing to do things contrary to his or her values in an effort to "fit in."

Have your group members share the things that make them feel different. The list could include being a Christian, being poor, having an alcoholic parent, or having a handicap. A situation such as the one faced in this Zinger is common for the older preadolescent young person. Activities such as scouting that young people found enjoyable as a child may label them as a geek or nerd as they get older. Allow the group to brainstorm possible solutions to difficult situations brought up by group members.

Additional Scripture:

1. How could Grant have handled this situation differently?
2. Why might Grant's friends think he is weird?
3. Why should Grant care what others think of him?
4. Why does growing up change the way you feel about some things?
5. How can you "fit in" and still do what God wants?
6. What should you do when "fitting in" means you must do something wrong?

High Points:

1. "Fitting in" becomes more important as you get older.
2. "Fitting in" becomes harmful when you do things that go against God's values.
3. Find ways you can "fit in," without sinning.

Scripture: John 18:15-27

Tell the group the story of Peter's three-time denial of Christ. Jesus had been arrested, and Peter had an opportunity to stand up for the Lord. However, his stand would have meant going against the crowd. Peter could have spoken up for Christ, yet in the face of pressure to conform to the crowd, he was silent. Peter compromised his faith in Christ to "fit in."

Additional Scripture:

John 15:19
Romans 12:2

A TYPICAL SUB-TEACHER TYPE DAY

When Brian walked into his classroom, he knew right away there would be a substitute teacher. The film projector standing in the back of the room gave it away. The only time his class watched films were Fridays or when there was a sub. Brian glanced towards the front of the room. Written on the chalkboard in large capital letters was the name "MS. FINKELSTEIN."

What a funny name for a teacher, he thought.

The day turned out to be a typical substitute-teacher-type day. During the filmstrip everyone threw spit wads, and one kid snuck tape onto the teacher's seat. The girls were passing notes left and right. Ms. Finkelstein's face got redder and redder as she got more and more frustrated.

At recess Brian suggested to his friend Terry that they switch seats. "You be Brian and I'll be Terry," he said. "It'll be a riot!"

So after recess Brian and Terry traded seats. Things were going great until Melissa told on them. Melissa was a notorious tattletale. Ms. Finkelstein looked furious. She sent the two boys off to the principal. But not before she gave the whole class a lecture.

"I've never had a more miserable day of substitute teaching," she said. "If I have my way, I'm never coming back here."

Was Brian right or wrong? Why?

Was Melissa right or wrong? Why?

Was Ms. Finkelstein right or wrong? Why?

A Typical Sub-Teacher Type Day
Leader's Tips

Topic: Showing off

Purpose: To examine showing-off behavior in young people.

Background Brief:

Preadolescents are known for their pranks. Pranks can be great fun, and there is nothing wrong with an innocent prank, but often pranks can get out of control. When they hurt others or intrude on the rights of others, pranks become a serious problem. Often we rationalize that preadolescent fun at the expense of others is normal. Unfortunately, this can reinforce negative acting out, which can lead to more serious delinquent behavior in adolescents. Young people need to see the difference between innocent fun and a harmful prank.

Read your group the following list of situations and let them decide if each is an example of innocent fun or a harmful prank. You will find that many of these situations can be either harmful or harmless depending upon several variables. Often, what a young person thinks is innocent really turns out to be harmful.

1. Turn the classroom clock ahead to get out of school early.
2. Shoplift on a dare.
3. Hide a water balloon in a friend's shoe.
4. Push someone off the monkey bars.
5. Tell a funny joke.
6. Tease someone about having a boy/girlfriend.
7. Pretend you are blind while walking around the mall with a group of friends.
8. Pass a note in class.
9. Tease someone who is wearing a leg cast.
10. Hide someone's lunch box.
11. Pull a seat out from under someone about to sit down.

Additional Questions:

1. Why do young people need to have fun?
2. Why do young people like pranks?
3. What are things kids can do to get attention without getting into trouble?
4. How can Christians have fun in a way that no one gets hurt?

High Points:

1. God expects young people to "live it up."
2. Having fun need not be at the expense of others.
3. If someone is hurt because of your fun, you need to make things right by apologizing.

Scripture: Romans 15:2

God asks us in this passage to keep others in mind when we decide to do something, for our actions affect others.

Additional Scripture:

1 Corinthians 10:23-24
Galatians 6:2
Philippians 2:4-5

GOING ROUND AND ROUND

When Tommy stopped going with Eva she was hurt. After all, he was the cutest, most popular boy in school. They had been together for three days. During that time they had held hands and talked on the phone every night. He had even kissed her after school.

Eva's thoughts were interrupted by her friend Barbara. They sat together every day at lunch.

"Eva, where are you? I've been talking to you."

"I'm sorry," Eva said. "I was just thinking about Tommy." She sighed.

"Tommy! I thought you were going with Scott now," Barbara said, wrinkling her nose in confusion.

"He's a nice guy and everything, but he's just not Tommy," said Eva.

Eva had agreed to go with Scott after she and Tommy broke up. They had been together a couple of days. Scott wasn't as cute or popular as Tommy, but he really treated her nicely.

"Hi, Eva."

Eva turned, and there was Tommy. He looked great.

"Could we talk? Alone."

As he said the word "alone" Tommy looked over at Barbara. She took the hint.

"I'll see you after school," she said to Eva as she left.

Tommy sat down beside Eva. Her palms began to sweat. *What could he want?* she wondered.

"Eva," Tommy began. He smiled at her. "I know you've been hanging around with Scott, but I'd really like to get back together with you. How about it?"

He has a lot of nerve! First he dumps me, and now he wants me to dump a nice guy like Scott, she thought.

Eva wanted to say no to Tommy, she really did. But as she looked at his face she began to think about the best way to tell Scott she couldn't go with him anymore.

Was Eva right or wrong? Why?

Was Tommy right or wrong? Why?

GROUP:_____

DATE USED:_____

Going Round and Round

Leader's Tips

Topic: Going together, opposite-sex relationships

Purpose: To help young people examine their opposite-sex relationships and the consequences of such early relationships.

Background Brief:

Young people today are getting involved in boy/girl relationships at increasingly younger ages. The upper elementary grades is not the place you would think kids would be "going together" (kids may call it something different in your area---"being together," or "going out"), but unfortunately in a growing-up-too-fast world, this is becoming more common. Even if most of your kids have not been involved in an opposite-sex relationship, they are still watching with interest their peers who are involved. The onlookers may think going together is stupid, or it may spark their interest in the opposite sex.

Early relationships tend to trivialize "going together" and what it means to have a relationship. At this age a couple who "go together" are only with each other for a few days to a few weeks. But what seems harmless really can be quite destructive. Kids are experiencing intimacy in these relationships, from evening talks on the telephone to holding hands and kissing. As they progress through relationships, they will tend to become more intimate with each relationship. As you can see, this can encourage sexual relationships by early high school or even late junior high.

Use this Zinger with a sex education unit or as a separate discussion starter to talk with your group about what having a relationship really involves and what that commitment means.

Additional Questions:

1. What would you do if this happened to you?
2. How many people do you know who have "gone together"?
3. How old should a person be before she or he goes with someone else?
4. What are the benefits of being involved in an opposite-sex relationship?
5. What are the disadvantages of "going together"?

High Points:

1. Opposite-sex relationships are important.
2. Getting overly involved in opposite-sex relationships at a young age creates problems later. You are tempted to become too intimate too soon.
3. You can find ways to have opposite-sex friendships without "going together."

Scripture: 1 Thessalonians 4:1-8

Paul here encourages us to live our daily lives to please God. He reminds the church to continue in the instructions given by the authority of Christ. Included in that instruction are some directions related to male/female relationships. In verses 3 through 8, Paul reminds us of God's will for opposite-sex relationships. The watchword here is self-control. God wants the best for the preadolescent. Problems can be avoided later by not getting involved in opposite-sex relationships now.

Additional Scripture:

Ephesians 5:1-2
Colossians 3:1-6

NO NEWS IS GOOD NEWS

Mr. Gaines was handing back the language tests as the students left the room. Finally he called Angie's name. She hurried to the door and snatched the test without looking at it. Only when she got to her locker did she look.

There at the top of the page was a big fat red D.

A D! *How can I tell my mom I got a D on my vocabulary test?* Angie wondered.

Angie had been doing poorly in language arts, so her mother had spent three nights helping her review the words for this vocabulary test. Her mother had really tried to help, but Angie's mind kept wandering. Language arts was the most boring subject she knew.

Why do I need to know a word like potential? she asked herself. She dumped her books into the locker and took out her coat. Her mom would be so disappointed when she found out. But wait—why did she need to know? If Angie didn't bring the paper home her mother would never know. Sometimes her teacher did not hand back their test papers. Maybe her mom would believe that. She could just say she got a B and not show her the test paper.

Angie wadded up the vocabulary test and threw it in the trash can. As she walked home, she thought about the story she would tell her mother.

Is what Angie did right or wrong?

Why?

GROUP:_____
DATE USED:_____

No News is Good News Leader's Tips

Topics: Deceit, honesty, parents
Purpose: To examine the negative consequences of deceitful communication with parents.
Background Brief:
At this age, young people begin to conceal things from their parents. This move towards individuality is healthy but at times takes a negative turn when they question their parents' motives and their secrets are deceitful. Many preadolescents also fight feelings of inferiority. Like Angie in this Zinger, they are reluctant to admit their mistakes for fear of ridicule or punishment. The stress of getting good grades is another factor that adds to these feelings.

Deceit and dishonesty are obviously bad ways to cope with life. However, the preadolescent often uses deceit to deal with immediate problems. Use this Zinger to discuss the negative consequences of deceit. Also, look at the benefits of open and honest communication with parents.

Additional Questions:
1. Why are grades so important to parents?
2. Is it possible to be honest with parents all the time?
3. Is not telling parents the truth the same as lying?
4. Why is it sometimes easier to lie than tell the truth?

High Points:
1. There are times when lying seems the only way out of a situation.
2. Dishonesty leads to more dishonesty. You have to lie to cover up lies.
3. Honesty is more than the best policy. God wants it to be our only policy.

Scripture: Galatians 6:9
Here Paul challenges the Galatian church to continue to do the right thing. God is in charge of the future, and we can trust him to reward our honest actions.

Additional Scripture:
Proverbs 12:13, 19, 22
1 Thessalonians 5:21

NO WAY

No way! This was not supposed to happen. Not to me—Carrie LeFaber. Lots of my friends' parents have divorced but I never thought *my* parents would do such a thing. After all, they taught me divorce was wrong. "Christians don't get divorced." That's what my mom used to say. Well, my parents are good Christians, and we go to church every Sunday. Dad is even an elder. And they're still getting a divorce.

How could they do this to me? I can't believe they're being so selfish. I have feelings too. And what about Ben, my brother? What's the divorce going to do to him?

The divorce is going to ruin middle school next year too. Mom said we would have to move again. She never asked me what I thought first.

They must hate me; that's why they're getting the divorce. I must have done something wrong.

All I know is, I'm never getting married. And I'm giving up on God too. He's never around when I need him.

What would Jesus Christ have done if he had faced this situation?

How could Carrie do what Christ would have done?

No Way Leader's Tips

Topic: Divorce
Purpose: To help young people cope with the pain of divorce.
Background Brief:
Parental divorce is one of the most painful experiences a young person can face. They not only have to cope with their parents' separation but with all the other consequences of the event. Many young people must change living situations, schools, and friends. The economic status of the family often changes.

      The young person may experience a variety of emotions during this time, i.e., anger, sadness, or guilt. Many young people feel they are responsible for their parents' divorce. This is a tremendous burden for them to bear. At this time, the young person may have difficulty functioning and expressing their emotions. This could result in concentration problems, lower grades, fighting, or periods of depression.

      A young person going through this needs to know they have a safe place to share their feelings. They need caring adults and friends to support them at this time. Others in your group may have gone through this situation and can offer suggestions on how to cope.

Additional Questions:
1. Has this happened to anyone you know?
2. Who could Angela talk with about her feelings?
3. Should Angela tell her parents how she feels?
4. How can you support a friend going through the pain of a parents' divorce?

High Points:
1. Divorce is a sad experience for young people.
2. Divorce is not the fault of young people.
3. Talking with other Christians can help the hurt of divorce go away.

Scripture: Psalm 23
      Millions of people have found comfort from this psalm of David. Here God is the Good Shepherd (Jesus was also the Good Shepherd, John 10:11) who provides us with comfort and protection.

Additional Scripture:
Isaiah 41:10
John 14:27
2 Corinthians 1:3-4

THE NEW STEP-WITCH

"Marie, you have smart-mouthed me for the last time. Just wait until your father gets home."

My stepmother is at it again. Picking at me. Always picking at me. Just because I didn't have time to clean my room she yells at me.

Who does this lady think she is—bossing me around like that? She's not my real mom. She's just Dad's stupid new wife.

I wish I could go back to the old days. It was a lot easier living with Dad when he was married to my real mom..

When the divorce happened, I could have lived with Mom, but Dad got custody. So now I'm stuck living with this stupid stepmother and her dumb daughter. I have all these new rules and chores. I have to do my homework right after school. I can't have my friends over anymore. And anyone can tell that my stepmother loves her own daughter better than she loves me. Now I know why there are all those stories about wicked stepmothers.

What would Jesus Christ have done if he had faced this situation?

How could Marie do what Christ would have done?

The New Step-Witch Leader's Tips

Topics: Step-families

Purpose: To help young people living in blended families find hope and support.

Background Brief:

The increase in divorce has brought about the increase in step-families. With a blended family comes new problems. Each person brings his or her own problems to the family, plus together they create new ones. Custody arrangements, visitation rights, family finances, and new living arrangements make the adjustment to a blended family difficult for the preadolescent. Younger children appear to have an easier time adjusting to a step-family. However, older children find it particularly difficult. Many older children never fully accept the reality of the divorce, blaming themselves or wondering why the family broke up.

The step-relationship between child and new parent can be difficult to navigate. Many new step-parents experience the step-witch or wicked step-parent mentality. Step-parents often feel like they are on trial, their actions constantly judged by their step-children. Step-parents also feel forced to instantly love their step-children. The same in reverse is true for the kids. But this love cannot be quickly forced. Living with these new roles can be difficult and trying, as shown by the large proportion of blended families who experience a breakup.

Use this Zinger to give kids living in blended families a chance to air their grievances. The group can help them brainstorm solutions as well as show them support. Young people living with both parents can also benefit from this activity because they come to appreciate their family situation as well as learn to support their troubled peers.

Additional Questions:

1. Do any of you ever feel like Marie?
2. How does Marie's step-mom feel?
3. Who could Marie talk with about her concerns?
4. How could you be a friend to someone like Marie?

High Points:

1. Living in a step-family is difficult for kids and parents alike.
2. Do not expect instant love or the perfect family.
3. Talk to someone about your hurt.
4. Each group member can be a source of strength and support to other hurting members in the group.

Scripture: Philippians 3:12-14

Paul compares living the Christian life to being an athlete in training. Paul's goal was to be and live like Christ. Paul is quick to point out that he has not yet reached his goal of Christlikeness, but it is his *only* goal. Preadolescents can make Paul's goal their own.

Additional Scripture:

Malachi 4:5-6
Philippians 2:14-16
Colossians 3:20

IT'S NOT FAIR

My little sister Ramona runs the house. She's *always* getting her own way. She practically gets away with murder too. Like when she used those bad words, Mom and Dad blamed *me* because they thought I taught them to her. I didn't. In fact, I avoid talking to her if I can help it. Anyway, she didn't even get spanked when she said those words. I would have been whapped right away, no questions asked.

Just because I'm the older one they expect me to do well in school, be a good Christian, and set a good example for my sister. I'm even supposed to watch out for her at school. Who do they think I am — my sister's bodyguard?

You'd think I'd at least get a bigger allowance because I'm older, but no deal. Ramona even gets more money than I do. And she gets more attention too. It's just not fair.

What would Jesus Christ have done if he were in this situation?

How could Ramona's brother do what Christ would have done?

It's Not Fair Leader's Tips

Topic: Sibling relationships

Purpose: To brainstorm on how to get along better with brothers and sisters.

Background Brief:

Sibling rivalry is an occupational hazard of being a brother or sister. Any member of your group who is not an only child will attest to the facts and frustrations of sibling rivalry. Even you may still have unhealed wounds from past conflicts with your brothers or sisters.

Today sibling rivalry can be intense because more parents are giving their best ten hours a day somewhere other than the home. This leaves less energy for kids. Children must vie more zealously for parental attention.

Use this Zinger to give your group a chance to share their sibling rivalry stories as well as brainstorm solutions to particular problems.

Additional Questions:

1. Why do parents treat their children differently?
2. How many of you know kids who feel the way this boy does?
3. How many of you know kids like Ramona?
4. Is Ramona's brother wrong to feel the way he does?
5. Whom could Ramona's brother talk to about this problem?
6. What kinds of problems have you had with your sisters or brothers?
7. What are some of the good things about having a brother or sister?
8. How can brothers and sisters live together without fighting so much?

High Points:

1. Sometimes you will like your brothers or sisters. Other times you will not.
2. It is okay to have negative (as well as positive) feelings towards a brother or sister. (Feelings are not good or bad. It is what you do with feelings that counts.)
3. It is not okay to hurt your brothers or sisters.

Scripture: 1 Thessalonians 4:9-10

Sibling rivalry was one of the first problems discussed in the Bible. Remember Cain and Abel? The New Testament, however, compares Christian love to sibling love, hence the term *brotherly love.* There is the downside of sibling relationships, but also a positive side. Challenge your group members to *practice* love towards their brothers and sisters even if they do not always *feel* love.

Additional Scripture:

John 15:9
1 Peter 1:22
1 John 3:11-12

A MOSTLY MIDDLE-CLASS SCHOOL

There are basically three groups at my school. First, there is the "top" group: the really popular kids. Most everyone knows who they are. They dress right and know how to act, and usually they have an older sister or brother who is popular. If someone doesn't think a person in the top group is cool, it doesn't matter. The majority of kids decides who is going to be in the top group.

The next group is the "middle class." This is where most kids would say they belong. If you are in this group, you dress okay and try to be cool, but for some reason you are not popular.

If you are not popular or in the "middle class," then you are in the "last" group: the "nerds" and the "brains." You can get good grades if you are in the "top" or "middle class," but you don't make a big deal of it. If you are a "brain," grades are all you think about, and you're usually the teacher's pet. If you are a "nerd," you're just plain weird.

That is the way it is at my school. I am in between the "top" and the "middle" class.

What would Jesus Christ have done if he were at this school?

How could you be more like Christ at your school?

GROUP:_____
DATE USED:_____

Mostly Middle-Class School
Leader's Tips

Topics: Cliques, popularity
Purpose: To help young people with their struggles with popularity.
Background Brief:
When adults think of popularity, they usually think of the teenage years. However, the pressure to be popular has become an issue for younger kids. Upper elementary grade young people are being pushed into more intense social situations. It is not uncommon to find cliques in elementary and middle schools that parallel those of teenagers. By the age of twelve and thirteen, peers have become as important as parents. Social groupings are much more fixed than in the younger years, mimicking those of older youth.

      It is important that you allow your group to verbalize the frustrations they have experienced over the popularity issue.

Additional Questions:
1. Why are some kids more popular than others?
2. Why is popularity so important?
3. What cliques or groups are at your school?
4. What does someone have to do to be popular at your school?
5. What group at your school would Christ fit into?

High Points:
1. It is important that the group of friends you choose is a positive influence.
2. Choose a group that shares your Christian values.
3. Choose a group that cares about you.

Scripture: Proverbs 13:20
      This is a straightforward passage of Scripture that, if followed, would be a blessing to every parent of a preadolescent. Encourage young people to be part of a group that they believe Christ would want them to be like (because they will come to resemble the group they choose to associate with).

Additional Scripture:
Proverbs 4:14
Proverbs 7:24
Proverbs 18:24

SPECIAL DELIVERY

You are at school. Mr. Engle, your teacher, is in the middle of a science presentation on the effects of friction–pretty boring stuff. You have written a note to your friend Gina, two seats ahead of you. You did not sign it. You pass the note to Gina, but before it gets there the girl holding it, Pamela, is caught. The teacher assumes Pamela wrote the note and embarrasses her in front of the class. To make things worse, the teacher reads the note out loud. In it you said some unkind things about another person in your class. Your friends are mad at Pamela, not realizing you wrote the note.

If this really happened to you what would you do?

How did you decide what you would do?

GROUP:_____
DATE USED:_____

Special Delivery Leader's Tips

Topic: Gossip

Purpose: To confront the problem of gossip.

Background Brief:

There are many things in life we could use more of. But gossip is not one of them. It is a problem for young and old. In fact, it is such a problem that when you begin discussing it with your group you may find your session quickly turning into a gossip time. So beware! Keep your discussion focused.

Young people in the upper elementary and middle school grades gossip—and gossip a lot! And unfortunately, trivial and ridiculous as much of it is, gossip is believed. And that is why gossip is so dangerous. People get hurt!

Additional Questions:

1. How would you feel if you were the girl that was caught?
2. Was what the teacher did fair?
3. What would be the risks in admitting to passing the note?
4. Why does gossip hurt people?
5. How can you avoid gossiping about others?
6. What do you do when your friends gossip to you about other people?

High Points:

1. God never had anything good to say in the Bible about gossip!
2. Gossip is a sin.
3. Have the courage to say no to gossiping.

Scripture: James 3:5-6

In this passage of Scripture, James compares the harm that the tongue can do to a raging forest fire. Gossip may start out innocently enough between friends, like a seemingly harmless spark. But a spark can start a raging forest fire, and gossip also spreads quickly out of control until irreparable damage is done.

Additional Scripture:

Proverbs 11:13
Proverbs 16:28
2 Corinthians 12:20

R-RATeD

Everyone swears at your school–*everyone*. As far as you can tell, swearing starts about the fourth or fifth grade. Some kids even begin earlier, but by fifth grade everyone is doing it. Sixth graders even make up stuff by putting different swear words together even if they don't make sense. Kids think it's cool. You don't like swearing and you don't think it's cool. But everyone else thinks it is. And if you don't do it you won't fit in.

Parents tell kids not to use swear words, but they swear themselves. You have heard your parents and your friends' parents use bad language, and you hear bad language on TV and in the movies all the time.

The teachers are trying to do something about the bad language, but they can't do much more than complain and yell. You wonder if there's anything you can do to help.

If this were your school, what would you do?

How did you decide what you would do?

GROUP:_____
DATE USED:_____

R-Rated Leader's Tips

Topics: Bad language, swearing
Purpose: To talk with young people about resisting peer pressure to swear.
Background Brief:
Many adults would be shocked if they were privy to the conversations of nine-to-thirteen-year-olds. Unfortunately, however, foul language is no longer shocking to this age group. Depending on one's circle of friends, bad language is often the norm today.

This generation of parents would not have used foul language at such a young age. However, the media plays a large role in defining the type of language used. Young people learn through role-modeling, and today cable and videos—not to mention national TV—broadcast foul language that they would not have been exposed to a generation ago.

Help your group members realize that this type of language is inappropriate. Allow them to discuss the pressures that they face to swear.

Additional Questions:
1. How common is swearing among people your age?
2. Why do you think young people use bad language?
3. Do you think Christ swore?
4. Do you believe swearing is wrong?
5. How do you respond when people swear in front of you?

High Points:
1. There is no direct commandment in the Bible against swearing.
2. Young people who swear usually are trying to prove how grown up they are.
3. Foul language shows one's immaturity, not maturity.

Scripture: Colossians 3:8
Misuse of God's name (Exodus 20:7) is not, as many people believe, directed towards swearing. Rather, it is a commandment against the frivolous, disrespectful throwing around of the name of God. His name is special and must not be dishonored through inappropriate use.

Cursing as the Bible uses it means either a prophetic vision of coming doom or the consequences of sin.

God does, however, want our language to be wholesome and pleasing to him. In condemning filthy language, the apostle Paul is referring to all bad speech, from the inappropriate expression of anger to lying. Swearing can be included as part of this filthy language.

Additional Scripture:
Proverbs 16:24
Ephesians 4:31

GRADE TRADE

You are at school and your teacher has just announced that it is time for arithmetic. To save time on paperwork, the teacher has you trade your homework assignments and grade them at the beginning of the class period.

Today you are sitting next to a good friend. You trade papers and begin to grade. Your friend is doing poorly. You check off a lot of wrong answers.

While the teacher is explaining the grading scale, your friend asks you to change some of his wrong answers before you give the grade on the homework to the teacher. If you change the answers, your friend will get a B instead of a C.

If this really happened to you, what would you do?

How did you decide what you would do?

GROUP:_____
DATE USED:_____

Grade Trade Leader's Tips

Topics: Honesty, cheating
Purpose: To examine the practice of cheating.
Background Brief:
A common practice of teachers is to ask their students to exchange papers for grading purposes. The teacher reads the answers to homework or tests, and students grade their classmates' papers. While this grading method eases the out-of-class paperwork for the teacher, it offers numerous cheating opportunitites to students. Even if a student does not give in to the temptation to cheat for him or herself, often pressure is exerted from peers to cheat for another's benefit.

Many of your group members will most likely have been pressured by their friends to be "a little lenient" in their grading. The older the student the more likely this has happened. They may not have asked someone else to cheat for them, but they have probably been asked to change a math answer or correct a misspelled word on a spelling test they were grading.

Brainstorm with your group different ways to handle a grading situation like this without cheating. Then role-play this situation with your group. Ask for volunteers to play students and a teacher. The role-play should practice ways your group can say no to cheating and still keep their friends. Allow a number of the group members the opportunity to role-play saying no.

Additional Questions:
1. How can you say no to cheating for a friend and still keep the friendship?
2. What will people in your class think if you never cheat?
3. What would happen if you told the teacher what was happening?
4. What might happen to you if you were caught by the teacher changing an answer on a friend's paper?
5. How could you talk to your mom or dad about a situation like this?
6. How does God feel about this kind of cheating?

High Points:
1. Young people face intense pressure to cheat at school as well as at home with homework.
2. The older you get, the more pressure there is to cheat.
3. Cheating takes away the opportunity to learn.
4. Cheating leads to more cheating. Each time you cheat, it becomes easier to do it again.

Scripture: Proverbs 1:10-19
This passage of Scripture is ideal for this situation because of its focus on group pressure. The young people who are faced with the temptation to cheat for someone else or feel the class pressure to let someone else cheat for them are being "enticed," as verse 10 states. Point out to the group verse 19, which speaks about the consequences of "ill-gotten gain." Ask the group to name the consequences of cheating (bad feelings, not learning, displeasing parents, hurting God, lower grade if caught).

Additional Scripture:
Proverbs 14:2, 12, 14
Jeremiah 17:4-10

WHICH WAY TO HEAVEN

A friend's father, Mr. Lopez, died three weeks ago from cancer. The doctor said smoking cigarettes for so many years probably caused the lung cancer that killed Mr. Lopez.

Your friend's father, Mr. Lopez, did not believe in God or church, yet he was a very good man. He worked hard for his family. He never hurt anyone. He volunteered as a troop leader for the Boy Scouts, coached Little League baseball, and helped raise money for playground equipment for your elementary school. He was always nice to you. Once, when you did not have enough money for a hamburger at McDonalds, Mr. Lopez paid for you. He spent more time with his three kids than any other father you knew.

You invited your friend to Sunday school this past week. The teacher talked about heaven. Now your friend brings up the Sunday school talk and wants to know if his father, Mr. Lopez, went to heaven.

If this really happened to you, what would you say to your friend?

How did you decide what you would say?

GROUP:_____

DATE USED:_____

Which Way To Heaven? Leader's Tips

Topics: Heaven, salvation

Purpose: To provide an opportunity to answer questions about salvation

Background Brief:

Your group members are at an age when they gain new thinking abilities. With these new abilities they begin to think differently about God. Their concept of God is very different at eleven years old than at seven years old. Younger children see God as a parent figure and accept him because their parents say he exist. They attribute to God the same things they see in their parents: God knows everything, God loves, and God punishes. Older children move away from a concrete God and are able to abstract the concept of God. They can view him individualistically and are capable of a more personal relationship with him. The younger child will talk about heaven as a place his grandparents went, while the older child is able to believe in a heaven as a truth.

Your group members will have many questions about salvation, their relationship with God, the reality of evil, their friend's salvation, and what heaven will be like. Allow your group members the opportunity to ask the questions that are puzzling them.

Much of the questioning arises because kids at this age compare the beliefs they have been taught with those of their friends as well as the beliefs presented by teachers and the media. Young people at this age need to be given the opportunity to discuss their questions rather than simply be given "the answer" by an adult. Often dogmatic responses only lead kids to seek out the truth from other sources.

Additional Questions:

1. What is God like?
2. How does a person get to heaven?
3. Is being a good person enough to get you to heaven?

High Points:

1. God is clear when he states that salvation comes only through Jesus Christ.
2. It is God's place to determine who enters and does not enter heaven.
3. We can be comforted by the words of Abraham: "Will not the Judge of all the earth do right?" (Gen. 18:25, NIV).
4. You can have God's salvation by repenting of your sin and placing your faith in Jesus Christ.

Scripture: John 14:6

Use this opportunity to answer your group's questions about salvation as well as present the plan of salvation to the group. Be sure to allow time for group discussion of each question rather than your immediately giving the answer.

Additional Scripture:

Matthew 28:18-20
John 3:16-18

CUT LOWS

You are eating lunch in the cafeteria. You and your group are having a good time talking, laughing, and eating. Suddenly, he appears: the cut-low champion of the school. A cut low is when someone puts you down. It usually happens in front of other people and makes you feel like a real jerk.

Well, this guy can cut you so low you have to look up to see the ground. And today, you are his target. He starts letting you have it, and you feel the eyes of all your friends upon you.

If this really happened to you, what would you do?

How did you decide what you would do?

GROUP:_____

DATE USED:_____

Cut Lows Leader's Tips

Topic: Put-downs
Purpose: To help young people understand how put-downs affect self-image.

Background Brief:
Put-downs pose a constant threat to the preadolescent, for they assault an already shaky self-image. A young person's self-concept is formed through the feedback received by others. Put-downs provide a person with negative feedback that can only harm the self-concept.

Movies and television situation comedies have given new meaning to put-downs, portraying put-downs as funny and giving little thought to how they hurt others. Young people see the humor in media put-downs, and they often mimic the behavior.

Additional Questions:
1. Why do we put people down?
2. How do you feel when you are put down?
3. How can you support a friend who has been put down?
4. How do you feel when you put someone down?

High Points:
1. Put-downs can harm a person's self-concept.
2. Choose friends that build you up rather than put you down.
3. Spend time developing your relationship with God, the builder of self-image.

Scripture: Colossians 3:12
Put-downs so often are committed as an effort to gain attention from peers. If Jason can put Brian down, others will laugh at Brian, and Jason gets peer approval. The Christian need not seek such negative peer approval to build self-image. And if Christians are on the receiving end of a put-down, they need to remember that God's empowering presence will help them meet life's challenges.

The self-image of the Christian is built upon a relationship with Jesus Christ. Christians need not feel inadequate, because the Christian is one of God's chosen.

Additional Scripture:
Jeremiah 31:3
Matthew 19:19b
John 15:5
Ephesians 2:10

SiT DOWN AND SHUT UP

It happens at least twice a week. A couple of students light up a cigarette or a joint in the back of the bus on the trip home from school. There are so many students on the bus that the driver never knows about it, or at least never does anything about it. You have not worried about it before because you have always managed to get a seat in the front. But today you weren't so lucky. You are sitting in the back next to the group who smokes. And they're lighting up right now.

You stand up to move towards the front of the bus, but you hear the driver yell at you to sit down. You feel like telling the driver about the smoking, but that seems so uncool. Besides, the smoking group would kill you.

If this really happened to you, what would you do?

How did you decide what you would do?

GROUP:_____

DATE USED:_____

Sit Down and Shut Up
Leader's Tips

Topics: Smoking, drugs
Purpose: To allow young people to discuss the drug abuse that occurs around them.
Background Brief:

Most young people are not out smoking cigarettes or marijuana at the upper elementary and middle school grades. However, that does not mean they are not affected by others doing it around them. Your group members know peers and older youths who smoke, they see drug abuse on television, they read about alcohol and drug abuse in the newspaper, and they hear about older kids they know who drink and do drugs.

Young people need an opportunity to talk about and process information on smoking, alcohol, and drug abuse. You can provide that opportunity. They also need some guidelines on how to react to situations involving substance abuse. All of your young people will have stories of how cigarettes, alcohol, or marijuana have touched their lives, even if they have not used them.

Additional Questions:
1. Why would it be uncool to tell the driver?
2. Why would you worry about what kids doing drugs thought of you?
3. Would you support a friend who did decide to tell the driver?
4. If you could, would you get up and move away from the smokers?
5. How would parents react if you told them?
6. How would you react if it were your brother or sister doing the smoking?
7. How many kids do you know that drink alcohol or smoke cigarettes or marijuana?
8. How does Jesus want you to react to people who use alcohol or drugs?

High Points:
1. As you go through your school years, you will hear about and see people who smoke cigarettes, drink alcohol, or do drugs.
2. Not everyone is doing it.
3. The closer you get to people who smoke, drink, or do drugs, the greater the chance you will too.
4. Talk with your parents or a trusted adult like a teacher, Sunday school teacher, or counselor if you are confused about friends who smoke, drink, or do drugs.

Scripture: Ephesians 5:18

Explain to the group that nicotine, alcohol, and other addictive substances can control you. Ask for examples of how cigarettes, alcohol, marijuana, speed, or cocaine control people. Tell the group that there is a better substance than drugs, something that will give them a lasting high—the presence of the Holy Spirit in their hearts. Being controlled by the Spirit is infinitely better than being controlled by alcohol or drugs.

Additional Scripture:
Proverbs 20:1
Galatians 6:7-8
1 Thessalonians 5:6-8

STRANGER DANGER

You have heard it at least a million times: "Do not talk to strangers or go anywhere with someone you do not know." Now that you are older your parents are letting you go more places by yourself. You can also stay home alone for longer periods of time. So your parents worry about you and give you so many "stranger danger" lectures you could scream.

One day you are walking home from a friend's house when a car slows down beside you. A woman calls out to you. You have seen the car around the neighborhood several times before.

You walk a little faster, but the car keeps up with you. The woman leans over to you through the open window and starts talking. You try to ignore her, but you hear her talking about her small son who is lost. She says he is only two years old. He walked out the front door and now she can't find him. Asking you to please help her look, she motions for you to get into her car.

As you reach for the door handle you remember your parents' lectures about getting into a stranger's car. But this is someone who has lost her little boy! Wouldn't your parents want you to help her?

If this really happened to you, what would you do?

How did you decide what you would do?

Stranger Danger Leader's Tips

Topic: Stranger danger

Purpose: To help young people understand the need to be cautious when dealing with strangers.

Background Brief:

Preadolescents are at a stage when they are given more freedoms, such as being at home alone or out on their own more often. Because they spend more time alone or with their peers, they have more contact with strangers. Since parents are not always there to help them, it is important to equip preadolescents with the knowledge and skills they will need to deal with situations that involve strangers.

This issue may be confusing to young people, when after years of being taught to be "nice" to strangers they are now told to be wary of them. While we do not want to scare them, we need to give young people guidelines to follow when a situation involving a stranger occurs.

Additional Questions:

1. Instead of going with the woman, what else could you do?
2. Why do some people want to hurt others?
3. Why do parents and other caring adults talk so much about "stranger danger"?
4. Why is it not "rude" to avoid a person who makes you feel uncomfortable?

High Points:

1. Most people are good and will not hurt you, but some will.
2. Do not get into a car or go anywhere with a stranger.
3. Run away and call for help if someone tries to force you to go somewhere or do something you do not want to do.
4. Ask for permission before you go anywhere with someone other than your parents.
5. Do not be afraid to say no to anyone that makes you feel uncomfortable.

Scripture: Psalm 89:2, 8

Since you have spent much of this session focusing on the need for caution when dealing with strangers, this is an ideal time to contrast the failings of people with the faithfulness of God. People may fail us (hence the need for caution), but God will never fail us.

Additional Scripture:

Psalm 36:5
Psalm 119:90
Lamentations 3:23